Phyllis C. Smith
1981

④

Phyllis C. Smith
1981

"**...Yet** *to every generation these come duly down . . . as if God brought them written in His hand.*"

Emerson did not have quilts in mind when he wrote these words, but he could have. Mrs. Willis Cameron of Montgomery County, Texas, and her granddaughter, Virginia Lee Adams, are shown with two of Mrs. Cameron's heirlooms. Generations of love — an enduring bond of time past, present, and the wonderful challenge of creativity that will be Virginia's tomorrow.

Southern Living

Award Winning Quilts

Effie Chalmers Pforr

Copyright © 1974 by Oxmoor House, Inc.
P. O. Box 2262, Birmingham, Alabama 35202

Southern Living Books

Award Winning Quilts

Editor: Candace N. Conard

Design: Sankey 2, Inc.
Photography: cover: Taylor Lewis
          text: Pat Peacock, Gil Barrera, Joe Benton
Pattern illustrations: B. J. Johnson, Steve Logan
Family Living Editor, *Progressive Farmer*: Felicia Butsch

Library of Congress Catalog Card Number: 74-80235
Manufactured in the United States of America
Fifth Printing 1979

ISBN: 0-8487-03561-1

To those gentle women throughout time who have made this life we live just a little bit warmer and a lot more beautiful, through the untiring industry of their hands and the abiding love in their hearts.

From the Scrapbag, 1

Of Beds and Quilts and Love and Such, 3

Love's Labor Found, 42
    Quilt-as-You-Go, 54
    Quilting on a Frame, 61

The Love Patches, 67

Acknowledgments
    Award Winners, 177
    Honorable Mentions, 177

Bibliography, 182

Index, 184

From the Scrapbag

When we were in the process of researching the fascinating world of quilts, a surprised library assistant remarked, as we checked through the line with our load of books, "Well, you sure have your work cut out for you."

"How's that?" we asked.

"Well, if you're going to make a quilt, you sure do."

"Why so?" we asked.

"Because it's a lost art," he said. "Nobody takes the time to make a quilt any more."

Contrary to his and others' misconceptions, women are quilting today. *Progressive Farmer*'s Quilt Block Contest brought forth thousands of entries from thirty-three states, and for those who were fortunate enough to see the beautiful quilt blocks on display, it was an exciting and memorable happening.

It is impossible to date precisely when quilting began. Vestiges of this art, a form of needlework where padding is stitched between two layers of fabric, indicate that people were quilting hundreds of years before Christ, and there is reason to believe quilting will exist, in some form or other, centuries after our generation has departed. For there are certain truths that never change: man is creative, and man thrives on beauty.

Quilts, although born of necessity, were the conception of love and the fruition of hours of labor. The results continue to be works of unbelievable beauty. The joy of personal expression that came to a woman as she created her quilt might have been termed "folk art" or "primitive," but art it was. This love, labor, and creative sense kept her tirelessly at her quilting frame and endlessly tutoring her young to count threads. Thus the art of quilting was carried on. The quilts were a legacy of love from one generation to another.

Such creativity continues. *Award Winning Quilts* is a compilation of the work of those women who have taken up their quilting needles to create. There are quilts of the past and those yet to be made.

Whether the quilt that you make is for yourself, for some bride's hope chest, or a love blanket for a little newborn, we hope *Award Winning Quilts* will bring you many happy hours.

And sleep warm.

H*onor the Women, they weave and spin heavenly roses in our earthly life.*
Johann Wolfgang von Goethe

Despite the ravages of time, this old Pennsylvania quilt still mirrors the hours of love that went into all those tiny stitches. Deep blue with a yellow cotton backing, the tulip quilting provides a perfect background for the bright appliqué. From the collection of Miss Ima Hogg, Winedale Inn Properties, the University of Texas at Austin.

*Of Beds
and Quilts
and Love
and Such*

Of Beds...

"The bed comprehends our whole life, we were born in it, we live in it, and we shall die in it," wrote Guy de Maupassant in the nineteenth century. Essentially he is saying that the bed encompasses our stay on this earth, serving as a silent companion for our journey.

One can only surmise how earliest man prepared his bed. No doubt nature was his Great Provider, giving furs for warmth and dried leaves and grass for a pallet.

In Bethlehem, Mary wrapped little Jesus in swaddling clothes (perchance quilted) and laid him in a straw-filled manger.

King Henry VIII, fretful volcano that he was, made certain his bridal bed would be a warm one when he married Catherine Howard, for he gave her some twenty-three quilts as a wedding gift.

Moving to another time and another place, we find that beds and bedding were of the gravest importance. When William Tecumseh Sherman's men came out of the North to ravage the South, some of the prize objects that were stolen by his army were the quilts that belonged to Southern women. One might well imagine that a lawless Union soldier, not having a decent bed of his own to sleep in, would not be above poaching a lady's quilt to die under.

History is filled with accounts of famous beds and bedding. And it is no different today, for we are born, celebrate life, and we die, and for each ceremony we need a warm and loving place.

A remarkable feature of fifteenth century beds was their size, for many were built to accommodate a number of people simultaneously. A late fourteenth-century Apocalypse tapestry in the cathedral of Angers shows a bed occupied by four men. And Albrecht Dürer, on his journey to the low countries in 1520, claimed to have seen a bed large enough for fifty persons in the Hotel de Nassau in Brussels.

In spite of their size, beds of the past were movable commodities. In the fifteenth century, beds were held together by pegs and could be taken apart for transport. Noblemen took their furnishings and hangings with them to and from their many residences, so, of necessity, beds had to be easily dismantled.

Mary, Queen of Scots was said to have taken twenty-five new beds and eleven old ones to Scotland when she returned there to govern in 1561. One has only to read the Scottish inventory of that year to visualize the beauty of the bed hangings, for they not only insured warmth for the royal blood, they also excited a feeling of aesthetic pleasure for the royal eyes. Mary's bedding was made of silk damask, velvet, taffeta, and cloths of gold and silver. The trimming for the valances was of gold and silver lace stitched with gold and silver thread. According to records, these accoutrements were beyond the power of mortals to describe.

Though the records concerning Mary's bed are rather detailed, little is recorded about her husband Lord Darnley's bed in the Kirk o' Field house. A gunpowder explosion didn't lend itself to inventory, and it's safe to say that after such a blast, all of the queen's seamstresses and all of the queen's embroiderymen couldn't put poor Darnley or his bed together again.

At Versailles the boudoir took a more hospitable turn, for there ladies received their friends at times when congratulations or condolences were in order. And by the "enlightened" eighteenth century, guests gathered in the bedroom or "salon" of Paris's renowned hostesses to discuss matters of intellect and poetry.

Such amenities were necessarily lacking in the lives of early American settlers. A broadside first printed in London and now displayed at the Smithsonian Institution warns emigrants of some inconveniences they will find in the New World:

Advice to Settlers 1622
The inconveniences that have happened to some persons which have transplanted themselves from England to Virginia, without provisions necessary to sustain themselves, hath greatly hindered the progress of the Noble Plantation. For prevention of the like disorders . . . it is thought requisite to publish this short declaration.

In the particular that followed, the broadside stressed the need to have "ells of Canute to make a bed and boulter, one rug for a bed," and ells of coarse canvas to make a bed for two men to be filled with straw. For the colonial women of New England and their frontier sisters on the parched prairies of Kansas, the bed was often the only piece of furniture with which they set up housekeeping.

The Four-Poster, a play by Jan de Hartog, uses the bed as the central stage prop. This homey comedy, spanning some thirty-five years in the lives of a couple, ends with the wife saying to her husband: ". . . it was a very good bed . . . I mean, it's had a very nice history, and that . . . marriage was a good thing."

A correlation may be drawn between the bride of *The Four-Poster* and the woman emigrating to the New World. A wilderness was to be her home, her four-poster represented her worldy possessions, and her faith in a new life was her husbandman.

 Our American ancestors did not underestimate the importance of beds. Consider the number George Washington was said to have slept in. One can calculate that, mathematically if nothing else, it would have been a humanly impossible feat for one man, however great, to have put his body in so many places at the same time.

And yet there is one bed for certain that Washington slept in. It stands in the master bedroom of Mount Vernon, surrounded by an aura of glory and covered with a magnificent quilt — once white, now yellowed with age.

Not all men of stature slept in beds as glorious as Washington's. Lincoln's birth bed was made of cornhusks and bearskins and probably had the aroma of a stable. At twenty-three, as part owner of a store in New Salem, Illinois, Lincoln slept in a wooden bed covered by a worn quilt and housed in a lean-to, a simple frontier structure.

But Lincoln prospered, and upon becoming president moved to bigger and better beds. An eight-foot bed was custom-made to accommodate the new occupant of the White House, although he never slept in it. Like the Illinois slim he was, he had come a long way from the cornhusks and the bearskins. Yet life was to leave him as it had found him — on a small, borrowed bed in a tiny room.

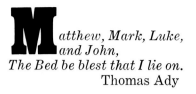

atthew, Mark, Luke, and John,
The Bed be blest that I lie on.
Thomas Ady

There's little doubt that this beautiful walnut tester bed (circa 1857) is blessed, for it graced the Texas home of the John Calvin Justice family for many years. From the collection of Miss Ima Hogg, Winedale Inn Properties, the University of Texas at Austin.

Whether a manger in a stable, a couch of silver in a house of state, or a cot in a lean-to, beds were important items in the lives of those who have gone before us.

Bedding for our American ancestors depended on available resources and a woman's ingenuity. What could not be hewn from the land had to be brought from home. Food was there for the taking, but wool and flax were absent. The pioneer woman brought her "ells of Canute," her scrapbag, and her dreams.

That this woman came to a forest primeval did not mean she had come from a primitive forest. She left countries that had been civilized for centuries. And although lifetime treasures were left behind, memories, experience, and a sense of adventure required no shipboard room.

One of her most valued possessions was her scrapbag. Fabrics were nearly as precious as life, and, adhering to the age-old admonition to "waste not, want not," she made certain every scrap of material was put to use.

Viewing an exhibit of nineteenth-century quilts sponsored by the Smithsonian Institution's Traveling Exhibition Service, a man was overheard saying to his wife: "My word, Nell, take a look at the patched spots on the patches of this quilt . . . . Those women didn't waste a thing, they used everything they had. That's what made this country so strong."

It was only natural that our American foremother, no matter from whence she sailed, would utilize all she knew from that which had gone before her. In beginning a new life, whether in the bustling streets of Boston or the lonely lanes of Kentucky, she remembered the things of beauty she had known in another time and place, and as the evening sun shone over her new home, she reached for her scrapbag and her needle — and God saw that it was good.

The art of quilting, American or otherwise, came into being because man needed it to survive. Quilting is thought to have begun in Egypt during the time of the pharoahs. Some of the Egyptian kings wore quilted garments that were made by obviously skilled craftsmen. Many artifacts remaining today not only support this theory, but also give evidence that the Egyptians were extremely advanced in textiles and dyeing. Even the Bible tells how the long years spent by the Children of Israel in Egyptian servitude left their imprint, for when the Israelites made their exodus, they took Egyptian knowledge of textiles, dyes, and embroidery with them.

The Chinese and tribes from the cold regions of Mongolia wore quilted clothing to protect themselves from the elements, as did inhabitants of India and Greece.

Possibly the most complete knowledge of the existence of quilting stems from the time of William the Conqueror and the Crusades at the end of the eleventh century. Returning Crusaders brought pieces of light quilted silk which the Moslems wore under their chain armor.

By 1400, quilts and quilters were a part of Eastern civilization. In fact, a famous ivory diptych, Milanese in origin, dating from around 1400 A.D., shows figures of the Holy Family in flight into Egypt. Joseph is wearing a quilted coat.

Climate doubtlessly contributed to the growth and acceptance of quilting, for turbulent weather marked the first half of the thirteenth century; unusual cold and snow plagued the early part of the fourteenth century. Quilting may have become a way of life by virtue of its own credentials, but when pushed to the fore by bitter climate it became the bread of life.

As centuries passed, quilted clothing and bedding were used in castles of the nobility and cottages of the peasantry for similar reasons. Quilting was universal for bedding, for children's caps to keep out the cold and agues, and for their parents' waistcoats or petticoats.

Because of the fragility of cloth, whether hand-woven or machine manufactured, quilts were not long-lived. For what mice and men did not destroy, moth, mildew, and mischief laid waste, and

*O*r standing long an oak, three
hundred year,
*To fall a log at last, dry, bald,
and sere:*

Ben Jonson

Probably no other pattern has
stirred so many hearts as *Log
Cabin.* This old quilt is particularly
interesting because even though it
is made of cotton, the fabrics
appear to be fine wool and elegant
velvet. From the collection of
Miss Ima Hogg, Winedale Inn
Properties, the University of
Texas at Austin.

there are only a few quilts extant today on either
side of the ocean that predate the nineteenth century.

However, we do know that the earliest settlers
"clouted," for one settler defined the process in "The
Forefather's Song" about 1630:

And now our garments begin to grow thin,
And wool is much wanted to card and to spin.
If we can get a garment to cover without,
Our other in-garments are clout upon clout.
Our clothes we brought with us are apt to be torn,
They need to be clouted soon after they're worn.
But clouting our garments they hinder us nothing;
Clouts double are warmer than single whole
  clothing.

One of the many reasons the earliest settlers fled
England was that the sheep were pushing them
off the land. Much of the common land was being
fenced in and used as graze land, for wool
manufacture was England's third largest industry.
When people no longer had land to till, they had
to find it elsewhere. And if sheep were pushing people
from the land in England, it stood to reason that
ships bringing people to the new country would not be
bringing sheep. Thus the new settlers had no
animals and they had no wool. The simple equation
worked out to "clout upon clout," reusing materials
until they were exhausted, hoarding the
precious scraps in the bag until there were enough
left over from patching clothes to make bedcovers. It all circled back to necessity.

But sheep finally came, and the settlers took their
flax and wool, their heavy looms and spinning wheels,
and created materials for clothing and bedding.

Of course, the fabrics were dull and their colors
were those of the earth: gray, brown, and blue with
an occassional Turkey red from madder (a root
yielding a red dye). But in many colonies these colors
were in tune with the tenor of the times —
a somber religion.

In other colonies women remembered the gorgeous
chintzes the East India Company used to bring
into Europe. They used their ingenuity and learned
the secrets of color from weeds, lichens, and
flowers of the woods. And they filled their scrapbags
with tidbits of treasured cloth.

11

It has been said that an American would never stand still long enough to let grass grow under his feet, and he is often portrayed as being in a terrible sort of hurry to get somewhere. This may well be true: witness the seemingly short time from the log cabin of the early settler to the plantations of the gentleman farmer: how few winds blew between the time the Father of our Country wore a uniform of rough wool to the time his knee and shoe buckles were of the finest silver.

And yet, short as it seems on history's pages, one has only to look at the utensils of the early settlers to imagine how hard the row of living must have been to hoe, how long the road wound down to independence, to realize the incredible achievements of our New World ancestors.

For one thing, whether they settled along New England's stormy seacoast or on the trail of Virginia's lonesome pines, the areas were filled with rocks and savages and wild animals, and the abundant natural resources that determined the condition of life in the new country could only be wrested from the earth by individual enterprise. It was small wonder that the settler was happy to put his shoulder to the wheel, anxious to get moving, to make time march on so that he could move from his log cabin to his manor house.

The growth and development of our country was recorded by the needles of women as they pieced the love patches that became their quilts and bedcovers. Womanpower was not wasted. Every girl, from the time she was a small child, was expected to sew. For the well-born, there were the "Needlework and Embroidery Schools," and the early newspapers carried advertisements offering instruction for "young Gentlewomen and children in the fine works of Quilting and feather-work." For those whose lot in life had been cast in a smaller mold, there was a mother's knee and her quilting frame, and many a child of three was given a number of threads each day to pull so that she would learn to sew a straight seam.

Such labor had its rewards, for the social life buzzed around the quilting bee. Invariably, a woman held a bee when she had at least two quilt tops ready to be quilted. Stories are legion of romances that began when the quilting was done, and many a young woman, well prepared with a dozen dowry quilt tops, had to make ready her baker's dozen — her bridal quilt — following a particularly enjoyable bee. And many a young man could have joined Stephen Foster's refrain to sing, "And 'twas from Aunt Dinah's quilting party, I was seeing Nellie home." Many hands made light work, and also made the romantic pickings more delectable for the young males who gathered at the bees.

But before the quilting bee there was a cutting bee which enjoyed equal importance, for it was here that patterns and gossip were exchanged. Without the bees (harvesting, barn-raising, corn-husking, cutting, and quilting) to bring the news from afar, life would have been incredibly barren. The socials were looked forward to with excitement. The women shared homemade loaves, freshly caught fish, and dearly hoarded patches. Consequently, many of the quilts were much alike, identifying a definite period and place in the history of quilting.

As the continent developed, so developed the history of the patchwork quilt in America. Some of the more knowledgeable, in recording the history of the American patchwork quilt, have divided its development into chronological periods ranging from the seventeenth to the twentieth century. This has been an admirable idea, for classical scholars have found certain thoughts, expressed in symbols, sewn into those early creations that allowed them to date the quilts, thereby tracing in no small measure what was going on in America.

An example of the benefits that could be derived historically from categorizing quilts into periods can be found in the revolutionary period quilts of Moses Richardson of Springfield, New York. These New England quilts of deep blue homespun were made from the same material as an old wool coat from the Revolution, found recently in a country attic. Upon the coat's breast was sewn the Purple Heart,

This pieced and appliquéd quilt (circa 1830) from the William Alston Plantation in South Carolina, is a perfect example of a framed medallion quilt. The layers of frames are modifications of the early chintz designs originating in the late eighteenth century. By the 1820s, specially designed chintzes were being printed in England for the center motif. Museum of History and Technology, Smithsonian Institution.

Your benefices twinkl'd from
afar,
*They found the new Messiah by
the star.*

John Dryden

The *Star of Bethlehem* shines out at museum goers with
all of the mystery of the past, yet appeals to the artistry of
the most modern with its exciting "op" effects. From the
collection of Jonathan Holstein and Gail van der Hoof,
Smithsonian Institution's Traveling Exhibition Service.

14

given for uncommon valor to an unknown soldier by George Washington. Some two hundred years had passed, but the home-dyed indigo was holding its own with the homespun, as was the courage that went into that very special Purple Heart.

But the people of the times were not concerned with periods or creating history. They made their craft designs from whatever was at hand and lived simple lives unaware of the effect they would have on history.

Quilts could be categorized by borrowing truths of the Declaration of Independence: man seeks life (God), he defends his liberty (politics), and he pursues his happiness (nature and property).

Since these were people who were consummately religious (many fled the countries of their origin for the right to worship freely), consummately political (their life's blood depended on their political persuasion), and consummately in pursuit of happiness by seeking to conquer the American wilderness and establish rights to it, it was only natural that they should lend their interests to the efforts of their hands and hearts — the names of their quilts reflected all of this.

These were fundamentally simple, God-fearing people, and if they read in a scriptural passage, "Their bodies are buried in peace; but their name liveth forevermore," they took the words literally and tagged a name on their handiworks. Furthermore, the name of a quilt was important, for patterns were borrowed and they required an identity.

Neither Arabic nor Roman numerals lent themselves to giving quilts an identity, although one notable exception is *Order Number Eleven*, a now famous quilt pattern re-created by a woman in Missouri to take the place of her mother's best quilt which was stolen by jayhawkers during the Civil War.

Many of the patterns were bizarre, and often indigenous to people of a particular area. Many of them were interpretations and intentional plagiarisms. And yet, it is estimated that there were never more than three hundred different quilt patterns in use.

Thus quilt names mirrored the characteristics, collectively and individually, of early Americans.

Women found expressions of every emotion in the Bible and translated them into quilt patterns: *Job's Tears, Crown of Thorns, Star of Bethlehem,* and *World without End.* The Song of Solomon provided the sentiments for a young bride's quilt: "As the apple tree among the trees of the wood, so is my beloved among the sons." And she named her quilt *The Rose of Sharon.*

Quilts were a means of expression not only for religious sentiments but for politics as well. Tacit political persuasions manifested themselves in such quilt names as *Washington's Wreath, Whig Rose, Harrison Rose, Fifty-Four Forty or Fight, The Little Giant* (referring to Stephen A. Douglas and his debates with Lincoln), *Lafayette's Orange Peel, Steps to the White House,* and numerous others.

George Washington's position in the American political system was of such importance that *Washington's Wreath* was one quilt pattern that ultimately got "put in" the quilting frames of most patriotic women of the day, even though the variations on the pattern were legion.

One design that never varied, however, was that of a weeping willow bent sorrowfully over a tomb, for when Washington died an orphaned nation wept, and quilt patterns reflected its loss.

The Rising Sun, a pattern done in the blue and yellowish-red color of the Continental Army's uniform, mirrored the hopes of the people. Its name originated with a statement Benjamin Franklin made when Washington arose at the conclusion of a meeting and Franklin pointed to the president's black armchair with its design of a half-sun, brilliant with golden rays. "As I have been sitting here all these weeks," he said, "I have often wondered whether yonder sun is setting or rising. But now I know that it is a rising sun." Years later, during the time of a great religious revival, *Rising Sun* was changed by quilting an eight-point buff star in the center blue square, and it was called *Delectable Mountains,* from John Bunyan's *Pilgrim's Progress.* "They went then, till they came to the Delectable Mountains, . . . to behold the Gardens, and Orchards, the Vineyards, and Fountains of water. . . ."

According to most quilt historians, the first named American pieced quilt pattern was *LeMoyne's Star,*

Because the road is rough and
long,
Shall we despise the skylark's song?
Emily Brontë

Rocky Road to Kansas, made of cotton, dates from New Jersey around 1890. Upon close inspection, designs within designs appear in geometric perfection. From the collection of Jonathan Holstein and Gail van der Hoof, Smithsonian Institution's Traveling Exhibition Service.

named for the two LeMoyne brothers who established colonies on the Gulf Coast following the explorations of LaSalle in that part of the New World. This old New Orleans pattern was the basis for more than a hundred star patterns, and from it comes *The Peony*, pronounced "piney," and all the tulip and lily patterns. It was so popular that travelers quickly took it to the English colonies on the Atlantic coast, and by the time the pattern reached the East it had undergone so many dialect variations that it bore the name *Lemon Star*.

As an illustration of the possible confusion of names and patterns, a slight change in the *LeMoyne Star* design resulted in a new pattern called *Yankee Pride*. It is easily understood by any Southern girl who has ever encountered William Tecumseh Sherman in the pages of a history book why the name was changed to *Dove in the Window*. After 1860 there was no place on any Southern woman's bed for a quilt named *Yankee Pride* or "Yankee" anything.

The world of commercial enterprise cast an influence on quilt makers, too. Patterns reflected the blacksmith with his anvil and forge, the carpenter with his saw and hammers, and the shipbuilder with his wheel and compass.

Patterns were also created in response to nature, with birds, animals, and meadows. If a bear was rumored to be in the vicinity, the pattern was *Bear's Paw*. If the ducks were out, waddling across the road, the quilt pattern was *Ducks and Ducklings*. If the wagon trip West was perilous and rugged, the quilt pattern was *Rocky Road to California*. And if the wagon happened to be heading down the Wilderness road, the name could just as easily have been *Rocky Road to the Ohio's Falls*.

Even recreation, limited as it was, came in for a full bow. Dances found their way into quilt patterns in *Hands All Around, Eight Hands All Around, Buck'n'Wing,* and *Swing in the Center*.

Everything that was any part of a woman's life in the New World — all of the pieces, light and dark, all of the unalienable rights, stated and unstated in her dream of independence — were reflected in the names she gave the children of her hands.

There were other facets of life which left an imprint on the patchwork quilt, pieced or appliquéd. The indelible personality of the people left its mark on the handiwork of its womenfolk. Just as people were identified by accent and dialect, quilts were identified by patterns and colors.

The Dutch and the Germans settled in New York, New Jersey, and Pennsylvania, but of all the American quilts, those of the Pennsylvania Dutch were the most colorful and the most intricate. Such characteristics were anomalies, for of all the women of the New World, these were the ones whose lives were the most circumscribed.

But the colors of their quilts were riotous, and the craft of their needles so intricate that women from other sections of the country were hesitant to copy the Dutch patterns. Such designs simply required too much time and effort. It could well have been that the colors and craft were a subtle rebellion against a drab lot, for the Dutch hands were calloused from labor, and their feet knew everything but the grace of an evening dance.

Quilts of the South characterized a different way of life. It has long been taken for granted that the Southern woman presents a stereotype of the refined, elegant plantation mistress so often identified with *Gone With the Wind*, and when one examines those early quilts of the Southerners, these characteristics could certainly be assumed to be true. The quilts of the Southern women were as native to them as their accent, and the lace they wore in their dress was copied in the patterns of their quilts. Their needlework was exquisite and the materials and patterns they chose spoke of a life of leisure and elegance.

The main characteristic of New England quilts was durability, for this was the hallmark of their lives. Stemming from the earliest days, when the scrapbag resembled Old Mother Hubbard's cupboard, the quilts were probably brought over on the ships and had been patched and repatched. Since the American pieced quilt really had its origin in utility rather than beauty, the earliest surviving examples are those made of linsey-woolsey, and these were the ones found in the Northeastern states. The majority of those still extant were made of whole cloth, and the back differed from the top. They were lined with wool, for the winters were cold and the living hard. The colors ranged from indigo, saffron, and madder to sherbet colors.

Two exquisite examples of New England linsey-woolsey quilts are housed in the Smithsonian Institution. The color of the top is indigo, and one is backed in a shining saffron. Both had been glazed, and both have intricate quilting patterns in swirls of flowers and baskets. Incredibly enough, they date from the time of George Washington.

When ships arrived from the English Trading Company bearing the cherished chintzes that could be cut and appliquéd, women rushed to buy them. Each little piece was given over to the scrapbag to await the day when a pieced quilt could be started. But such fine fabrics came later. In the beginning, the pieced quilt was heavy, durable, and ready for the hard life.

Of course, when the great movement West began, with its Conestoga wagons and its dreams of glory, a convolution of the sections was achieved, and Pennsylvania Dutch, Southerner, and New Englander melded into one gigantic crucible.

Antiquities are history defaced, or some remnants of history which have casually escaped the shipwreck of time.
Francis Bacon

These quilts from the collection of Jonathan Holstein and Gail van der Hoof are on display as part of the Smithsonian Institution's Traveling Exhibition Service.

20

The colonial period had given way to the days of the pioneer, and the story of the scrapbag repeated itself. For the farther west the wagons rolled, the farther away the availability of materials, and the pieces in the scrapbag became increasingly fewer and smaller.

Hawaiians added another dimension to the art of quilting. American missionaries brought their bibles and patchwork to the Islanders, and the magnificent new fabrics related to the brilliant colors of Hawaiian pineapples, fern grottos, waterfalls, and flower gardens. The result was an array of designs, mostly appliqué, that was entirely different from the American's folk art.

Quilt top designs cannot alone claim the laurels for the American quilt. Intricate quilting stitches and stitching patterns have been particularly outstanding on this continent. This phase of quilting may be admired as a work of art and beauty in itself. Quilting, rather than piecing or appliqué, demands a fine, experienced hand: the quilting stitches in a myriad of intricate designs determine which quilt is to become a collector's item.

Many quilting designs of the past were so unbelievably beautiful that the quilt could be reversed for equivalent beauty. Long before 1870, quilting alone was in such demand that a quilter's finest accomplishment was often executed in all white. A solid white quilt demanded greater imagination as well as skill, for without the aid of color, quilting became doubly important.

Examples of the fine art of quilting could be seen in quilts from the Smithsonian Institution's Traveling Exhibition Service.

The premise of this spectacular exhibit was not to show fine needlework, but rather to show the quilt as a forerunner of contemporary painting trends such as "op" effects, serial images, use of color fields, negative space, mannerisms of formal abstraction, and so on. The quilts were displayed like paintings so that viewers could see that even in these old quilts, pattern and color were consciously arranged to gain an overall effect that was artistically pleasing, often achieving geometric perfection as well.

One quilt in particular abounded in white-on-white patterned blocks, and each one had a different quilting design, ranging from a snowflake to a star to a Maltese cross.

In another quilt, a *Double Irish Chain* pattern from Maine, circa 1890, the border alone was a masterpiece. Carrying out the same timing and counterpoint as its main theme, it made a veritable symphony out of what had started out as an ordinary, everyday quilt.

In viewing these museum heirlooms, one automatically examines the quilting needlework, so fine as to appear to have been mechanically done. It would have been one thing if the quilting had been done by machine, but to realize that it was done in a running stitch with an ordinary needle, the left hand under the quilt and the right hand sewing, with no control save that of the quilter... well, words fail. To make one was a monumental achievement; to own one, a priceless experience.

Quilting patterns which covered the background in and around the larger pieced designs were elaborate. Feathers, fruit, birds, bouquets, cornucopias, baskets of flowers, pineapples, shells — anything and everything — could be bought and stamped on papers, if a quilter had a mind to buy. Straight quilting, such as diamonds or cross-bars, was achieved with a ruler and pencil.

Continuing the credo of waste not, want not, a quilter often resorted to "teacup quilting," whereby she just took a handleless teacup and drew overlapping circles to guide her stitches. However, the stitching designs for most quilts required a great deal of proficiency, and many quilters used stamped papers and stencils.

These manifold designs were divided into two main groups: plain and fancy. The "plain" group included the horizontal, cross-bar, double cross-bar, diagonal, diamond, and double diamond quilting designs. The "fancy" group was divided into two sections: block and running. Among the most popular "block" designs were the feather wreath, widening circles, spider web, and wheel of fortune.

"**A**nne, sister Anne, do you see anybody coming? And her sister Anne replied, "I see nothing but the sun which makes a dust, and the grass looking green."
Charles Perrault

Anne Harbert of Birmingham, Alabama, treasures this magnificent *Crazy Quilt* — a gift of love passed down through four generations.

This colorful old appliquéd quilt is a good example of the style often associated with a special occasion or a particular organization. The insignia is thought to be that of an Odd Fellow Lodge. From the collection of Miss Ima Hogg, Winedale Inn Properties, the University of Texas at Austin.

The most popular "running" designs were the teacup, running vine, and princess feather. In England, the quilting patterns (called "filling" patterns) were fairly similar to the American, and for a very good reason: most of the American designs had come over from the mother country.

Regardless of whether it was English or American, designed with a teacup or by a professional pattern-maker, quilting patterns were of primary importance to a quilter, for by using tiny stitches, she held together, in a decorative manner, the three layers of material that comprised a quilt.

Fashion played an important role in the designs of quilts, for whatever styles of the day were popular, so those styles showed up in the needlecraft.

Originally, the "crazy quilt" was made from mad scraps of any and every material from the scrap-bag, cut to all sizes, and designed in such a manner so as not to waste the tiniest patch. But as time passed, and the colonist's lady became the colonel's lady, her scrapbag was filled with velvets and silks and ribbons of satin, and her "crazy quilt" took on an air of elegance and refinement.

The "friendship quilt" was just what the name implied: the woman who made it used materials given to her by her friends. The quilt could be all of one pattern, or it could be really interesting when each block, equal in size, boasted a different pattern. During the Victorian era, the "friendship quilt" became the "mourning quilt," and there was a veritable rash of these monstrosities.

One "mourning quilt," described by a young librarian who had seen it in a museum in Kentucky, had a graveyard as its center design, tombstones and all, with a border of black coffins. From the story that was told about this sepulchral oddity, the woman who made it apparently moved a coffin, like a chess piece, every time a relative passed away. It was said that she had even embroidered the names of the relatives on their coffins, causing quite a stir in the family.

"Freedom quilts" were quite in vogue for a while. They were fun quilts to make and were given to young men when they reached their twenty-first year. The only quilts made especially for men, they marked an important time in the lives of youths who, reaching legal age, were freed from parental control.

The "medallion quilt" enjoyed some degree of popularity, especially in New England. As the name implied, it was a quilt that had a medallion for its central motif. In many instances the medallion commemorated a special occasion.

Perhaps the best known of the "medallion quilts" is the one attributed to Martha Washington. It has for its center scene "Penn's Treaty with the Indians," a piece of an English copperplate-printed cotton. It is said to be a rather ordinary illustration of the medallion-type quilt, but it manifests the combination of the appliquéd, pieced, and bordered designs that were characteristic of this style.

Apparently the style was more popular in England than in colonial America, and its popularity could be attributed to the type of material needed for the medallion. It was much easier to get rich, expensive material in England where one didn't have to pay a king's ransom for it.

Another style that was quite the model in its day was the "presentation quilt," which was really a form of the "album quilt," and was popular from the 1870s to the early 1900s.

The "presentation quilt" was usually made by a congregation for the minister, or by members of a lodge for the retiring president. One such quilt of this type, owned by Mrs. Willis Cameron of Montgomery County, Texas, is the "Circuit Rider," made in 1901 by the Methodist Church women of Troy, Texas, to raise money for their circuit-riding pastor. Names of the supporters were embroidered in red on the spokes of the wheel, and, at $.10 a name, over $400 was raised. A close examination of this very special old quilt shows some names embroidered in black. These were the deceased members whose names had been restitched.

Since the church was such a vital part of the social life of women, it is easily understood how the "album quilt" could have originated. There were so many occasions to make one; there were so many oppor-

The love of liberty is the love of others;
The love of power is the love of ourselves.

William Hazlitt

Dated 1860, this rare liberty quilt from Pennsylvania exemplifies the type quilt given to a minister and his wife or presented to a visiting dignitary to symbolize a feeling of appreciation, well wishing, and affection. In one block is the American Shield, and in another, a wagon embroidered with the words "Northern Liberty." From the collection of Miss Ima Hogg, Winedale Inn Properties, the University of Texas at Austin.

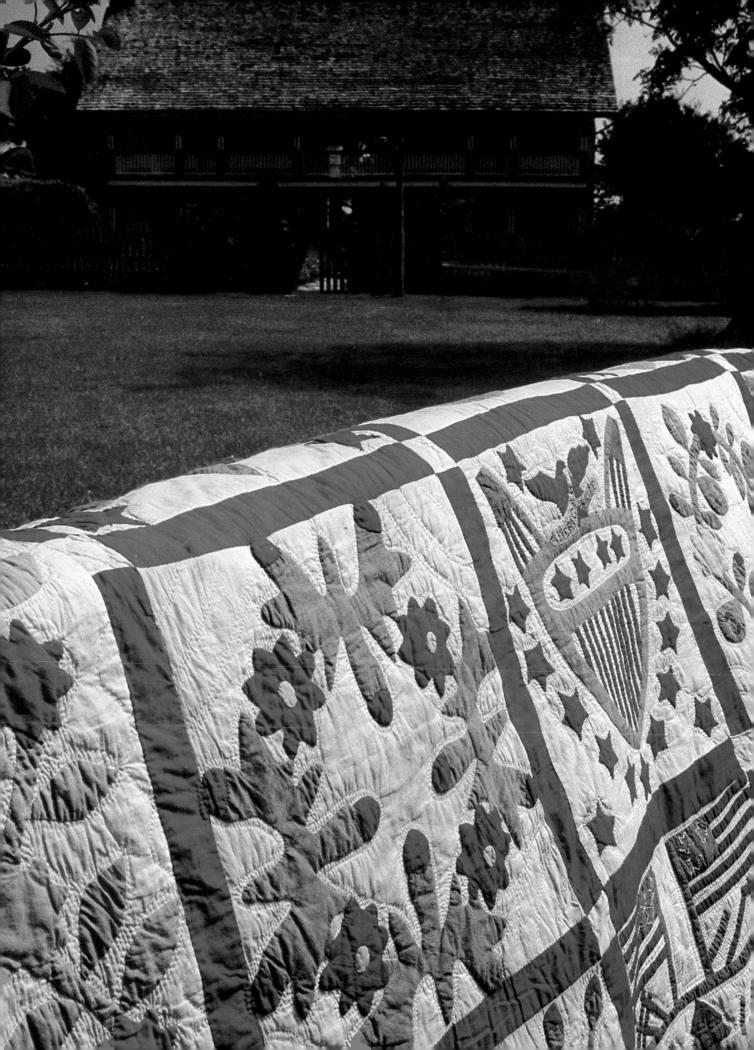

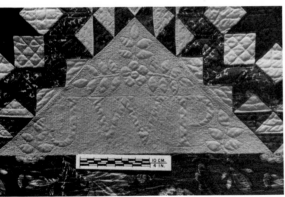

tunities to give one, with all of the love and the messages that these tokens of affection carried.

Usually, an "album quilt" consisted of blocks made and signed by a number of persons. Consequently, the blocks differed, but each was signed by the person who made it. Many times, if the person for whom the quilt was being made was moving away, there would be freehand messages embroidered onto the block, and the words, along with the gift, conveyed the feelings of the quilters.

Again, as in so many events that were a part of our ancestor's lives, the making of the "album quilt" meant that women — and men, for they added their names too — got together for a common purpose and thereby enjoyed the camaraderie of a shared gift.

Not all "social" quilts were made by groups. Church and state fairs brought quilters out to show their handiwork and compete for a blue ribbon.

Few social diversions were embraced with such enthusiasm. If women vied within their small groups for recognition as superb quilters, how much more they strived to take blue ribbons when placed in competition with women from other churches, and other counties. As the years passed, it was an eagerly anticipated occasion when one could enter a quilt, along with jams and jellies and livestock, in regional expositions such as The Eastern States Exposition at Springfield, Massachusetts, in which were exhibited the finest work of one's hands, and the harvest of one's fields.

There is no question that county, state, and even world fairs aided the art of quiltmaking. It wasn't unusual to see a man taking first prize for a hand-woven coverlet, but it was the women who took the prizes for bed quilts.

The community influence of the quilt could not be overestimated. For proof, one need go no farther than the Folk Festival in Kutztown, Pennsylvania. The festival still brings quilt enthusiasts from near and far, and, as in 1874, the familiar patterns

Jane Winter Price of Maryland made this pieced quilt in the *Carpenter's Wheel* pattern between 1825 and 1850. Museum of History and Technology, Smithsonian Institution.

28

and traditional motifs are the most highly
prized quilts.

A church bee, a county or world fair, a magazine's
quilt block contest: each furthers the art of
quiltmaking.

People have been superstitious from time imme-
morial, and the early Americans were no exception.
Often seen on quilts were such marks as the hex of the
Pennsylvania Dutch; the pineapple, symbol of
hospitality; and the tulip, an omen of good luck. And
heaven forbid that a young girl make a quilt
that had hearts on it if a young man was not on the
immediate horizon, for so anticipated, he would never
appear and spinster she would remain.

Quilters were careful not to break a thread while
quilting, for that could only mean an evil hour
was approaching. And no one should make a perfect
quilt, for that would be an offense against God. This
alone caused many an otherwise perfect quilt to show
up with an irregular, out-of-place block.

Quilts embodied the moods of the times, and as
obvious as they were in many quilts, they were just as
subtle in others. If the days were halcyon, the quilts
were as gay and bright as those of the Pennsylvania
Dutch. But if there was a sadness or war upon the
land, the quilts reflected the somber mood.

The nineteenth-century quilts displayed by the
Smithsonian Institution's Traveling Exhibition
Service show the depth of despair that gripped our
land during the years when the country was locked

A *land . . . where the light is as
darkness.*
The Book of Job 10:22

This *Log Cabin* quilt, a
fascinating example of the "light
and dark" block arrangement, was
made of wool in Pennsylvania
around 1860. From the collection
of Jonathan Holstein and Gail van
der Hoof, Smithsonian Institution's
Traveling Exhibition Service.

in battle, North against South. *Log Cabin*, made in 1860 by a Pennsylvanian, bore witness to the sadness by blocks arranged in a "light and dark" pattern. In its strings (the pieces are too small to be called scraps) are seen hardship and tears mixed with artistry. To feel the rough woolen lining through the poverty of the fabric brings to mind the image of a woman bowed by misery.

There are those who believe that the pieced quilt had its heyday between the years 1750-1850. There are those who think that the Civil War sounded its death knell.

One authority felt the Victorian era dealt the mortal blow. This era saw the colonial pieces of classic design thrown into the attic and the new, machine-made furniture move in. It saw the once treasured handmade quilt being termed "common," and the bedspreads of solid white from the Jacquard looms sparkling up from new brass beds. It was no longer considered fashionable to make a quilt.

Another quilt authority blamed its decline on the birth of such novelty quiltmaking as *Fanny Fan* and *Horse Shoe*. She felt that women were striving so hard to come up with different designs that instead, they succeeded only in destroying quiltmaking as an expression of feminine creativity.

Quiltmaking might well have weathered all of these storms had it not been for the machinery which nullified the need for handwork. It is interesting to note that if the height of the American pieced quilt was from 1750-1850, the decline began simultaneously with Elias Howe's introduction of the sewing machine — a machine so simple in its construction and action that it could be worked by a child. By 1855, these wonderful machines were becoming quite a popular addition in homes, and by 1880 more than a million had been sold.

It certainly should not be difficult for us, living in the last quarter of the twentieth century, to comprehend why a woman would forego the endless toil of piecing and quilting by hand, when she could achieve the same effect (almost) by sewing on a machine. Women got tired, that's all, and they welcomed the chance to lay aside their patterns and quilting frames. They wanted to enjoy their new freedom, their new-found opportunity for an education, their victory over what had heretofore been the shackles of domesticity.

There is no doubt that in America's yearling days most people slept warm under quilts and hand-woven coverlets, and there is little doubt that the majority of American women quilted. Throughout the nineteenth and into the twentieth century, seventy-five percent of America's bedcoverings were quilts.

In the new world of the sewing machine, the steam engine, and that brightest ray of all, electricity, there was no longer any need for women to hone their needles and save their scraps. They had finished the sixth day and could rest from their work.

In 1886, a black farm woman from Athens, Georgia immortalized her impressions of the Old and New Testaments in this now-famous *Bible Quilt*. Museum of History and Technology, Smithsonian Institution.

...And Love...

The most incredible thing about a quilt, whether heirloom or newly made, is intangible. The artistry of the design may be spellbinding, the superb craftsmanship may announce itself like a blare of trumpets, and the beauty of the pieces may evoke memories of days past, but it is the eternal quality of love that makes a quilt. No one ever made one, and no one ever gave one, without giving of themselves.

A quilt has an incredible power to evoke loving memories in people, notably among men. A high executive in a large public utility firm got downright sentimental when the subject of quilts came up. "I have at least ten of my mother's and grandmother's quilts," he said, "and there isn't a night I go to bed that I don't sleep under at least one of them."

An art director for a large publishing house, upon coming across a photograph of a *Little Dutch Boy* quilt while putting together a book on quilts, said, "Why, this is the same kind I had on my bed when I was just a little bit of a fellow, back on the farm."

An executive editor of a home magazine, checking a layout for a quilt article, said, "You know, my mother could have left her four granddaughters any number of things. But she made certain each granddaughter had one of their grandmother's quilts."

It has been written that Dwight Eisenhower, when he was president, was asked to indicate a quilt that he would want designated as "his" quilt, and he chose *Baby Blocks*, for this quilt pattern brought back many happy memories of his childhood in Kansas.

Mrs. Richard M. Nixon has been given a number of beautiful quilts, but one that stands out is *The Cherry Tree*, a quilt made by two women in the Appalachian area and given to Mrs. Nixon from the Save the Children Foundation's Appalachian Fireside Crafts.

The Cherry Tree pattern was found in the rafters of an old house in the Southern mountains, but the colors and stuffing of the cherries are the interpretation of its makers, Mrs. Dollie Bowling of Ricetown, Kentucky, and Mrs. Berta Hensley of Booneville, Kentucky. The quilt is appliquéd with green leaves and thirty-eight dozen stuffed cherries, all worth 144 hours of work.

Mrs. Delbert Mann, the former Ann Carolyn Gillespie of Nashville, Tennessee, now residing in

Beverly Hills, California, treasures two quilts: "One my mother made for me, the other she and I made together and the pieces are scraps of material from all the dresses she made for me over the years, for she always made all of my clothes up to college days, and each piece of the quilt recalls a dress to me." Ann writes, "It was quilted by two little old ladies in the mountains of Kentucky, who, when they returned it, apologized for the high price, $2.36, but they had had to buy another spool of thread."

Quilts embody lives — the courage, the character, the beauty, the humor, the music, and the art, all sewn right into each quilt and passed down through generations. Small wonder that the immortality of love a quilt evokes reaches out to us from the past.

Many of these heirloom quilts are extant because they were considered "best" quilts. A woman would only bring out her "best" quilts when she had guests or when the circuit-riding minister was due. These were the quilts that were spared the hot afternoon sun and were carefully laid away in blue tissue paper, away from the hustle-bustle of daily living.

Many of these "best" quilts were made during a time when quilting was no longer as necessary as it once was. Marseilles spreads and other machine-made covers, and homes that were larger, warmer, and better built, made the pieced quilt superfluous. Most of the quilts ceased to be used, and, fortunately, some of them were put away, thus carefully preserving the love and labor that had gone into them.

Museums the world over are possibly the greatest, most appreciative repositories of "best" quilts, for they take these priceless art objects, protect and cherish them, and at the same time share their wealth with the public. There, the ravages of time are at a minumum.

For anyone interested in the history of quilts, a visit to the Museum of History and Technology at the Smithsonian Institution is a must. The Hall of Textiles houses the early beginnings of quilting as an art form in America, as well as its demise with the Jacquard loom of 1840 which precipitated the all-white Marseilles spreads.

Of the many quilts in this wing, the first to catch the eye is the "Rebekah Hale Harris Bed Rug, Connecticut, 1776." Rebekah made for her dowry

John Hewson's skill as a textile printer is evident in this intricate block print. Made around 1800, the design adorns the center of a cotton quilt top. Museum of History and Technology, Smithsonian Institution.

chest this coarse, nappy piece of needlework in shades of mustard yellow and dark green against a beige background. In 1778 she married Lt. Joseph Hale and became a sister-in-law to Nathan, the famous American patriot.

A quilt to closely observe in the exhibit is *"The Bible Quilt."* Using the same fabrics of which many quilts of the period (1886) were composed, an elderly black woman from the outskirts of Athens, Georgia recorded with familiarity and affection her view of the highlights of the Old and New Testaments, from the Garden of Eden to the Crucifixion of Christ.

An eternity could be spent describing the various scenes depicted in the blocks of this quilt, but the more impressionable details are the nails in Jesus' hands and feet and the hair "pieces" of Adam and Eve and Cain's wife. The hair is made of triangular patches giving an almost halo effect to each figure. Recognizable in the quilt are patterns from other quilts: *Star of Bethlehem, Crown of Thorns,* and others.

A quilt of historical significance is "Indian Painted Cotton 1725-50." This museum piece is particularly interesting because it dates from the time when to be caught with cotton meant loss of life or limb, for its production and importation were illegal, and the courts of England were not above removing a head or a hand for breaking the law.

Important in the area of design is the "Hewson Quilt Top, circa 1800." The block-printed motifs appliquéd to its center square are typical of designs by John Hewson, one of America's first textile printers. An Englishman persuaded by Benjamin Franklin to settle in America, Hewson set up his print works in Philadelphia before the Revolution. Despite British attempts to eliminate competition by suppressing American textile printing, Hewson succeeded in developing his skills as a foremost textile printer. His success prompted the British to offer a reward for him, dead or alive. They were unsuccessful, fortunately, and the Hewson family rode in the Grand Federal Procession in Philadelphia on July 4, 1788, celebrating the adoption of the Constitution, and George Washington reportedly pointed with pride to the Hewson fabrics worn

Mrs. W. A. Odom (left) and her daughter, Mrs. Myrtle Stevens of Pumpkin Center, Alabama, put the finishing touches on a gorgeous *Double Wedding Ring* quilt top just before quilting it.

by Mrs. Washington.

The many facets of quilt love are confined neither to museums nor to the past. Letters which accompanied the quilt blocks shown in "The Love Patches" express the sentiments which have kept, and will continue to keep, quilting a time-honored art. Beatrice Gladys Baker of Zebulon, North Carolina, wrote:

Only a few weeks earlier I had discarded some old quilts which had been in hard service since the 1800s. It seems terrible. They were not museum quality to start with. They had been made strictly for use, not for display, and they had been used for every imaginable purpose: pallets for that childhood treat, sleeping on the floor, and for the littlest ones to crawl around on; to wrap wagon loads of tobacco going to market, and, incidentally, to soften the rest of the farmer who stayed at the warehouse with his product overnight; to cover bushel baskets of sweet potatoes in freezing weather and, most exciting of all, to fold into a thick pad on top of the ice cream freezer so that some lucky child could sit atop it and hold everything down for a few last turns of the crank. Actually the quilts had earned a rest . . . .

And so quilting has become a meaningful experience for me. It keeps alive some of the best of the past and helps to give that feeling of putting down roots which all of us need, whether we realize it or not. [A quilt] produces something which continues into the future, allowing us to give incalculable pleasure to others. It provides an outlet for artistic instincts at all levels, from copying to creativity, and allows a feeling of accomplishment at all levels. After all, a quilt is a quilt, whether it is thrown together to keep out the cold or patched and completed with an artist's skill. It serves practicality, even beyond the generally accepted definition of that function, by giving color and light and personality and character to the surroundings. And if all this does not count, it does indeed offer something to do for those who need it.

No matter who says it or how it is shown, a quilt *is* love.

Beth Gutcheon, who writes, teaches, and designs, finds a deep humanness within old quilts, and feels that if they could talk they would tell tales of "months of mindless, thankless tedium, cooking food of a depressing sameness, washing and sewing and mending clothes that were forever being worn out or outgrown, frustrating days and sleepless nights with a whining child...."

Patchwork, according to Mrs. Gutcheon, is the blues of the American woman: "The blues as a musical form was created by and for suffering — the blues is the feeling and the blues is what makes it bearable .... Patchwork became both the symptom and the cure for what life demanded of the American woman." Perhaps the American patchwork quilt has been overly romanticized, perchance even petted too much. Nevertheless, this romance is reality.

In Pumpkin Center, Alabama there lives a family of quilters. Mrs. W. A. Odom and her daughter, Mrs. Myrtle Stevens, quilt every day of their lives.

Back when the girls were small (there were six girls and six boys, the four oldest being girls), the depression was on and Mr. Odom was lucky: he had a job as a miner, making fifty cents a day. But there were all those mouths to feed, and the food had to come from somewhere. And it did, from their small farm worked by the girls, the wood chopped by the girls for their wood-burning stove and fireplace. They labored early in the morning until late at night, and then they gathered around their quilting frame and sewed.

Mrs. Odom, a sprightly 79, looks around the hills at Pumpkin Center today and says, "Yes, we were raised up hard, but I'm proud of what I've done. And my quilting has been one of the proudest things I've done." Her quilts reflect the love and care of that gentle woman whose life has not been gentle, and it is fully understandable how the patchwork quilt has become romanticized. For nowhere has it ever been written that romance meant freedom from sorrow or freedom from hard work and disappointment. Romances have been written because, in spite of all these things, love triumphs.

...And Such

The popularity of the patchwork quilt has risen and waned, yet now it is experiencing a renaissance. Look at the magazines for women and the home; go to the neighborhood library and try to check out a book on quilts; stop by a favorite bookstore and observe the number of available quilting books and the number of people buying them; visit a quilt exhibit and regard the myriad people who come.

Why are quilts so popular today? The need for free expression has surfaced: people are tired of the sameness that comes from the world of the ready-made. They want to create a visible expression of human experience. As Alvin Sella, associate professor of Art at the University of Alabama, has said: "The creating of art is the revolution of oneself through one-self. This sense of being part of a celestial and earthly harmony creates an urge to express it."

We are back to *Bear's Paw* and *Rose of Sharon* and *Job's Tears*.

But, with a difference....

Today's quilts are no longer objects of utility, but rather objects made for the sake of their handmade beauty. No longer confined to beds, quilts are a new art form waving as banners, appearing as soft sculptures, and hanging on walls.

Young artists of the seventies are giving new dimensions to quiltmaking. Ann-Sargent Wooster of New York typifies a new breed of quilters. As a sculptress, painter, and quilter, she feels that many of the young artists of today are finding a world of communion with "the women who created these incredible pieces of fine American folk art," and that they are relating to them better than to contemporary artists.

Ms. Wooster sees quilting as an extension of her sculpture. Her clear plastic quilt, "Stolen Cars," was made by painting three packages of toy metal cars a brilliant Chinese red. The cars were then heat-sealed into plastic using an iron and a ruler to make the lines, and finally the edges were bound in red tape. Had she used a lighter weight plastic, she could have quilted it on the sewing machine.

"Stolen Cars" was so named because painting the cars reminded Ann of stories she had read of secret workshops where stolen cars were repainted and given new license plates. Bowing to a quilting superstition from the 1800s, Ann placed a green car in the lower right-hand corner. She explains, "only God can create a perfect thing. If a human produced an object without flaw, it would call the Devil and misfortune would follow."

Another revolutionary quilt form is an interesting comment on social conditions. Amy Stromsten, also of New York City and a friend of Ann Wooster's, made a contemporary photographic wall quilt in which she took the traditional *Maple Leaf* pattern, piecing each maple leaf block from a different photograph which showed the abuse of the American countryside.

Patchwork, though off the bed, may still be utilitarian in a fashionable way. Patchwork has invaded shops (many handle patchwork items exclusively), in the form of dresses, handbags, beach towels and cushions.

Dorothy Weatherford, a Coty award-winning designer, promoted the Mountain Artisans and developed their home furnishing designs, receiving for her efforts an award in Home Furnishings from the National Society of Interior Designs. All this started as an altruistic effort: the creation of a non-profit corporation dedicated to opening economic opportunities for women of West Virginia.

The "renaissance" of quilting has never been used in a truer sense than in reference to the Mountain Artisans. A group of industrious quilters in West Virginia, they have brought new life and styles to quilting. For what began in 1968 as an effort to help rural women has turned into a great success. Reborn from what was originally a WPA failure, Mountain Artisans today has a large number of women who work in the cooperative, and each of them earns money for her work. According to Sharon Percy Rockefeller, who for the past six years has been highly instrumental in helping guide the enterprise, this money is supplementary income: "They use it to install indoor plumbing or to buy glasses for a child. Our purpose is to help these women economically without disrupting their lives." To widen the market for their products, the Mountain Artisans have added such items as tennis dresses, patchwork halters, and bridal clothes to their line of resort wear.

*There were twa sisters sat in
a bour;
Binnorie, O Binnorie!*
From "Binnorie"

The two sisters sitting in the bower of Corn Tassel, a craft shop where quilting is taught, are learning the craft. Pam (left) and Patty Lovelady are the daughters of the Richard Loveladys of Hallelujah Hill, Alabama.

Many other groups work in the marketing of quilt products. Such groups include: the Southern Illinois Quilters; the Martin Luther King Freedom Quilting Bee; the Storm Group from Whitehall, Illinois; and the Dakotah Handcrafts Group, of South Dakota. Amish women make and donate patchwork quilts to be auctioned and proceeds from the sales support the charitable work Mennonites carry on around the world. The Dakotah Handcrafts Group is of particular interest, for many of the quilters are Sioux Indians.

The Quilters of Miami Beach is an organization motivated by service, producing garments for needy children, often literally out of scraps. Begun by the Live Oak Sunday School class, income from sale of comforts and quilts has gone for purchase of hymnals or stained-glass windows for the church or, in earlier days, to help underwrite the pastor's salary.

The Quilters welcome visitors with words of fellowship: "Just bring your lunch and a thimble." According to the current president of the group, the class is two years behind in its quilt orders.

Such cooperatives and crafts groups are scattered throughout the country, and the ones named merely touch the surface of the innumerable community quilting enterprises in which women quilt for some degree of profit.

And for every group that is a large organization run with a sense of direction and purpose, there still remains that little church circle that gets together weekly to enjoy quilting and fellowship.

Jean Ray Laury's name is sheer magic in the world of quilts, for her designs have blossomed on the covers of every conceivable kind of home magazine. "Today," Mrs. Laury says, "our reasons for making a quilt are clearly other than practical ones. Quiltmaking offers enjoyment in the process itself as well as pleasure in the finished product. Quilts provide a lovely fragile and personal kind of silent, visual communication from one generation to others."

So no matter how it is said, or how it is sewn, that's what quilts are all about. And the pieces of that lovely, fragile and personal communication were and ever shall be, patched with love.

Love's Labor Found

So You Want to Make a Quilt

Mrs. George Steed puts the finishing touches on her gorgeous *Log Cabin* quilt pictured on the cover. She demonstrates how to create this pattern in the quilt-as-you-go method, creating a "light and dark" diamond motif.

After delving into history and seeing how truly beautiful many of the old quilts were, it is understandable that you would want to make an heirloom of your own. For that's just what your quilt will be — something to enjoy, and something to pass along (if you can part with it!).

The basics of making a quilt are pretty much the same as those of making a dress: what design do you want, where will you use it, and what suits your fancy? There are some other basics, too, the same as for any sewing project: pattern, fabric, needles, pins, thread, scissors, a ruler, a mind's eye picture of your finished item, and patience. Yards and yards of patience.

Two important tips before starting your quilt: First, look at a finished quilt that uses the pattern you would like to copy. This will help you with your design. It will help you in estimating yardage, placing your blocks mentally, and in your fabric and color selections. But this is not to imply that you can't enlarge upon a theme or change a design. Second, if possible, locate a talented quilter to help launch you in your new work. Nothing succeeds like success, and nobody knows more about how to make a quilt than a woman who has made a number of them. This is why we went to experienced quilters for patterns and instructions.

You will invariably meet the words "patchwork," "piece," and "patch." "Patchwork" describes any quilt pattern, whether the design is created by pieces appliquéd to a larger background fabric, by separate geometric shapes sewn together, or by a combination of both processes. In the chapter on quilting patterns you will find designs illustrating each of the three techniques of making a quilt.

"Pieced" (or "patched") designs are created by joining rather small geometric shapes to form blocks that are then set together to make a completed quilt top. Pieced designs are generally made up of squares, rectangles, triangles, diamonds, hexagons, or a combination of any of these shapes. To give your quilt variety, you may wish to alternate pieced blocks with plain ones. This gives you a stage on which to try your hand at fine quilting stitches.

A finished quilt has three layers: (1) the top, which is the design; (2) the filling (or batting), which is the center; and (3) the backing (or lining). The three layers are secured either by quilting — small, even, running stitches — or by tufting or tying, which is seen in quilts of an older nature, although some modern-day quilters use this method to make comforters.

If you choose an appliqué pattern such as *President's Wreath* or *North Carolina Rose*, the pieces are cut out and sewn to a background fabric with either tiny, microscopic stitches or decorative embroidery. You may buy commercial quilted material and use it for the appliqué fabric without having to do the actual quilting, and if you really want to try something exciting and different, select a pattern using the English style of padding. An example of this is *Oriental Bouquets*, which employs appliqué, padding, and crewel at its finest. You may even do your appliqué on the machine, using any number of stitches from zigzag to buttonhole. There simply are no limits to the ways appliqué may be treated.

Another suggestion for a beautiful appliquéd quilt is to cut out designs from patterned material such as chintz. The early settlers did this — when they could get their hands on some. Flowers and birds, as well as other designs, lend themselves to gloriously colored quilts.

For your first quilt, choose a pattern that will go with your decor and try to keep it simple. Next time you can attempt something as fabulous as *Flower Garden* or *Cathedral Windows*.

PATTERNS

There are several points to consider when choosing which pattern you wish to make, particularly if you are an inexperienced quilter:

(1) Squares and triangles are easier for a beginner than more complicated geometric designs such as hexagons.
(2) Patterns with curves should be avoided until you have mastered a simpler design.
(3) Designs with small pieces should be avoided until you have more confidence. Tiny pieces just make for bigger headaches.
(4) The larger the pieces of your design, the easier it will be for you to make.

These two stunning quilts from the repertoire of Mrs. George Steed, are as different in pattern and design as night and day. The *Cross-Stitch* quilt on the left demonstrates the beauty of the tiniest, most intricate design; the *American Glory* quilt on the right uses bright colors and large appliqué shapes.

COLORS

If we do not give a dissertation on color selection, it is simply because only you know what you want to achieve; only you know the colors that make you happy. An old, traditional design can take on new life by enlarging the design and using dramatic, imaginative color with such materials as ginghams, dotted swiss, colonial calicoes, or flowered prints.

However, before you run out and buy yards and yards of this or that, take the time to experiment a little. Take a lesson from the diagrams in the pattern chapter. Using a felt-tip pen or crayons, work out your color scheme before you start spending money.

FABRICS

Quilt Top — Your choice of fabric is a personal one. There are any number that make up into beautiful quilts, and you have a veritable world to choose from. The one thing to avoid is the combination of a heavy fabric, such as velveteen, and a lightweight fabric, such as dotted swiss.

Many quiltmakers think in terms of cotton or cotton blends. They are soft, easy to work with, durable, and the selection is endless. If you choose cotton, it is best to use a shirting or blouse-weight fabric that is both colorfast and preshrunk.

Contrary to what many quilters do, Mrs. Aurelia Venable, creater of *Grandma's Square* in the pattern chapter, never preshrinks her new material for she never washes a quilt. She sends her creations to the dry cleaners. However, if you should elect to make a crib quilt or one for a young child, you might put yourself ahead of the game by laundering your fabrics before you begin your quilt.

Gingham, broadcloth, polished cotton, percale, linen, muslin, blends of cotton, cotton satin, flannel, calico, satin, silk, velveteen, and cotton and polyester are all suitable for quiltmaking. If you buy new material, get the best you can find. It will pay off in the long run, for you will probably have your quilt for many years to come.

Filling — Filling (or batting) is available in either 100% cotton or in dacron polyester. A cotton filling tends to be thinner and does not hold up very well under heavy use and repeated cleanings. The polyester filling is probably easier to find and makes a nice, puffy quilt. However, the thinner the layer of filling, the finer and easier the quilting will be. Both types of filling are available packaged and precut in sizes 81″ x 96″, 81″ x 108″, and 90″ x 108″.

If your quilt is to be used in a child's room, you might find it wise to use a blanket as filling, for it is sure to be a good weight and able to withstand much wear and tear.

Backing — The fabric weight you choose for the quilt backing (or lining) should correspond to the type used on the quilt top. You may use brightly colored sheets or purchase 36- or 45-inch wide materials and piece them to obtain the desired dimensions. Backing fabrics of soft cotton are also available packaged and pre-cut in the same sizes as the filling.

YARDAGE

There are two things to consider when estimating the amount of yardage you will need: first, the size of your quilt; and second, your design.

It is taken for granted that you have decided which size quilt you are making: coverlet, single, double, queen, king, or a block or two for a throw pillow. The size will decide how much material you need for the quilt filling and backing. The pattern design will determine how much material you need for the quilt top.

To determine how much fabric is needed for your design, it is easiest to figure it in terms of color. Trace and cut from heavy paper a full-size pattern piece for each shape and color that you need for one block. Be sure to add a ¼-inch seam allowance to all sides of the paper pattern pieces before cutting them out; trace the pattern pieces on large sheets of paper 36″ x 36″, one for each color in your quilt design. Measure each traced sheet and estimate to the closest quarter of an inch. Multiply each color estimate by the number of blocks needed for the entire quilt top. If you plan to add anything extra, such as strips between the blocks or a border, figure that yardage separately.

CUTTING PATTERNS

Absolute accuracy is essential when cutting the fabric shapes if your creation is to fit together properly and appear uniform. To ensure a perfect patched block, you must have a pattern for each shape in your design.

Many patterns do not allow for seams, for some quilters prefer to add their own. Check the pattern instructions to see whether the pieces given include a ¼-inch seam allowance. If not, either modify the given pattern before making the template, or remember to leave ½ inch between each fabric tracing so you will add the seam allowance when cutting.

To construct the template, get some finely graded sandpaper (this gives you a strong template and one that won't move on the material) and using carbon paper, a ruler, and a pencil, transfer the cutting patterns to the sandpaper. Make sure the rough side of the sandpaper is the top of the design. (If you put two thicknesses of sandpaper together with glue it will give the pattern added body, thus making it last through many quilts of the same design.) After cutting out each template, be sure to label each pattern piece according to block design and size. By doing so, you will avoid confusion in the future.

If you encounter a problem with your design — and you could if it's your very first quilt — just remember that any design is merely a matter of arithmetic, and if those early colonists could figure things out when they had so few extra resources, it stands to reason that you can.

Should you wish to alter the size of your design, trace the pattern on regular graph paper before making a template, and count the number of grid squares required for each piece. Increase or decrease the size of each pattern piece by the same number of grid squares and the pattern should still fit together. You may wish to cut out the grid patterns and arrange them according to your design to be sure the pieces will fit together. This is particularly helpful with complicated geometric shapes, where the size is so important.

Mrs. Steed's magnificent *Lone Star* quilt (also known as the *Star of Bethlehem*) hangs from the staircase of an Alabama home. A colorful *Double Wedding Ring* is tossed over the bannister.

CUTTING FABRICS

(1) Get good, sharp fabric scissors and a small pair for clipping threads.

(2) Be certain your templates are accurate. A difference in the width of a seam can throw your entire design off.

(3) Iron your fabric and be sure the grain is straight.

(4) Place fabric wrong side up and the sandpaper template rough side down on top of the fabric.

(5) Leave ½ inch between each tracing if your template does not include seam allowances. Each piece then has a ¼-inch seam allowance and your drawing line becomes your seam line.

(6) Arrange the longest side of your pattern on the straightest grain. This will keep the pieces from puckering when they are sewn together.

(7) Place any appliqué stem pieces on the bias.

(8) Trace around your sandpaper template with washable pencil or tailor's chalk.

(9) Cut your fabric rather than tear it, particularly if you are a beginner, for this will help ensure piecing accuracy.

(10) Cut all pieces needed for the entire quilt top before beginning to sew.

(11) Group the cut pieces, keeping different colors and patterns separate. Doing this organizes your scrapbag.

You may wish to separate the blocks with strips and you may want to give your quilt a border. Strips between blocks can add much to an already stunning design. In the case of an appliqué, strips really set off the pattern, dramatizing the block with either a matching or contrasting color. Strips are also a means of making the quilt larger if you are in need of extra inches.

Borders are a must on many quilts, for it is the border that often gives a quilt its charm. Borders give an expert quilter a field on which to display her finest stitching patterns. Keep in mind that a border should be cut on the grain. Should you have to piece your fabric to get the correct length or width, the seams will show less if each strip is cut straight on the grain. Whether or not you separate your blocks with strips or add a border, the finished quilt will look best if it is finished as one would finish a picture — with a frame. Either bind it, edge it, or border it, but frame it.

PIECING

When creating a quilt made entirely of geometric shapes such as the various star patterns, piecing is impossible unless each shape is precise. Experienced quilters have pieced so many designs that accuracy is second nature to them, but a useful crutch for beginners is the paper technique often referred to simply as "papers."

Make the sandpaper template in the usual manner, except you will need two — one that includes a ¼-inch seam allowance and one that does not. Cut the the fabric shapes using the template with the seams allowed. Cut an equal number of newspaper shapes using the template without seam allowances.

Center the newspaper shape on the wrong side of the fabric shape. Fold the fabric seam allowances over the paper form and baste through the paper. Do this with every piece to be used in the quilt face. Each shape should now be exactly the right size and shape to fit into your design.

To connect each piece, place them right sides facing each other and whipstitch the pieces together with small, even stitches; press open. As each block top is completed, clip the basting stitches and remove the papers. Your block design is precise and sure to be equal to every other block on your quilt top.

If you are an experienced seamstress, you may wish to forego the papers and rely on your good eyes and steady hands to piece together the shapes. You may piece by hand or with a sewing machine. Geometric shapes are relatively easy to piece on a machine since the seams are generally in a straight line. However, sewing by hand gives you a better finished product if you need perfect seams and corners, and if you have sharp angles to turn.

The main point to remember is that whichever way you start piecing, whether with or without papers, by hand or by machine, you should make each block in exactly the same manner: start and end at the same point on each block to ensure a more accurate and uniform quilt top. After a few blocks, piecing will feel like second nature.

APPLIQUÉING

Fabrics chosen for an appliqué design should be not only beautiful, but closely woven so that a clean edge results when each piece is cut.

Make a sandpaper template for each appliqué piece, using the rough side for the top of your design. Trace according to directions, remembering to allow for seams if the pattern pieces do not already include them.

A great tip for smooth edges on appliquéd pieces is to machine-stitch all around the design outline (not seam outline). This makes edges much easier to turn, neater in appearance, and adds stability to your design.

Cut your appliqué design along the outside lines and clip the seam allowance along all curved edges and corners. Turn seam allowance to the back just inside the stitched lines and press flat. You are now ready to pin and baste your design onto the background. Slipstitch each piece into place with matching thread and tiny, tiny stitches.

QUILTING

Here are some general tips on quilting to consider before assembling your quilt:

(1) Use needles 5/10 betweens recommended by many quilters, or use No. 7 or 8 sharps, often recommended because they are short and make taking small stitches easier.

(2) Use a strong sewing thread — between No.'s 30 and 50 — always.

(3) Begin each seam with a small knot or backstitch, and end with two backstitches. Take a backstitch whenever the seam you are sewing crosses another.

(4) Make 5 to 9 stitches per inch, depending upon the fabric thicknesses. Stitch length on a machine should be set from 6 to 12 per inch. The closer the quilting stitches the stronger your quilt will be.

(5) Press the seams together in one direction, not open, as you finish a section of the block.

The beauty of appliquéd flowers is seen in two of Mrs. Steed's quilts, *Appliqué Rose* (left) and *Appliqué Iris*. Shown hanging from the doors of a large antique armoire, the quilts add beauty to the decor of any period.

You will have fewer layers of fabric to quilt through and the seams will be stronger.

(6) Sew the pieces by hand if they are small. Use a machine if the seams run long. You will find the sewing easier in both instances.

(7) Choose patterns which are sewn on the bias or diagonal when quilting on a machine. The fabric gives very little, thus making it easier to keep the surface flat while sewing.

(8) Run quilting lines approximately 2 inches apart for 100% cotton filling, and 3 inches apart for dacron polyester filling.

(9) Finish all of the blocks before you start to set them together. This allows you to check your design arrangement and see how your colors have worked out.

After careful planning on paper, quilting designs are marked on the quilt top only when all the blocks are complete and assembled. (Unless you are using the quilt-as-you-go method described below, in which case each block is quilted as it is assembled.)

Using dressmaker's carbon and a tracing wheel is the easiest way to transfer your quilting designs to the quilt top. Straight lines may be marked with sharpened tailor's chalk and a ruler, and quilting designs needn't be marked at all if you plan to follow specific lines which are evident through the patchwork or appliqué patterns.

Whether done on machine or by hand, quilting stitches are short, even, running stitches that can be made by two different methods: either take two or three short running stitches before pulling the thread through, or use the "punch" method — push the needle down through the three thicknesses in one motion and then back up again in a separate motion, close to the first stitch. With both methods hold the quilt firmly down and guide the stitches with one hand while quilting with the other. The thumb of the guiding hand is often taped to prevent soreness.

Quilt-As-You-Go — It stands to reason that if quilting as a folk art almost died out, the one sure way to be certain it is revived is to find a new approach. The quilt-as-you-go method, often called "apartment" quilting because it requires less working space, is just such an innovation.

For our source on this method, we went to a talented quilter, Mrs. George Steed of Lineville, Alabama. She was easily found, for her entries in *Progressive Farmer*'s Quilt Block Contest served as a beacon light, and when we called to talk about her beautiful *Pineapple* and *Flower Garden* patterns, she said, "C'mon down," and we went. The trip was well worth the effort, for we not only met a wonderful woman, but we also found the perfect person to tell you about quilting. Her quilts are jewels, each and every one of them.

Mrs. Steed likes the quilt-as-you-go method because she "goes" a lot, and she can either pick up a block or two and take it with her, or pick one up at random when she gets back home. When she does pick it up and completes a block, the block is just that — complete. It has a top, a filling, and a backing, and it is ready to be joined to another finished block. The quilt is on its way to being finished.

Mrs. Steed chose a backing of gold broadcloth for the *Log Cabin* quilt she is making in our demonstration photographs; the filling is dacron polyester. The prints and solids for the quilt top are of polished cotton for the most part, ranging from exquisite yellows, pinks, blue, and lavenders, to dark oranges, navy blues, deep purples, and sherbet pinks. The finished quilt appears on the cover of this book. Her *Pineapple* pattern lends itself to a similar treatment.

To prepare the block for assembly, cut the backing fabric into 9-inch squares (plus seam allowances). If the finished quilt is to run 90" x 108", you need 10 blocks across and 12 down (120 9-inch squares of backing). In buying her material, Mrs. Steed planned to bind her quilt with her backing fabric, so she allowed for the extra material.

Next, cut the dacron filling to fit the backing squares (120 9-inch squares of filling).

Finally, cut the squares for the center of each *Log Cabin* pattern and the material for the "logs" (retangular strips). The central square is approximately 1 inch (plus seam allowances), and each log measures about ¾-inch wide (plus seam

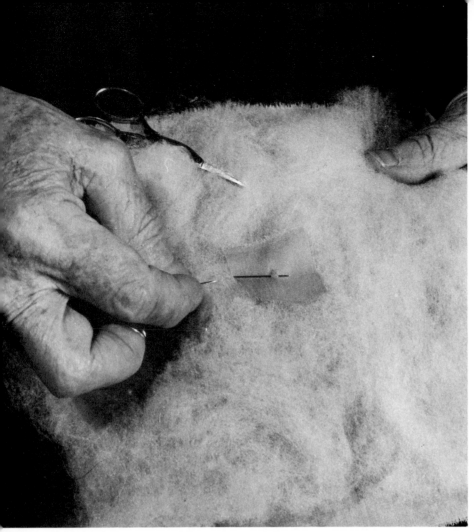

Pin the 1-inch center square to both the filling and backing.

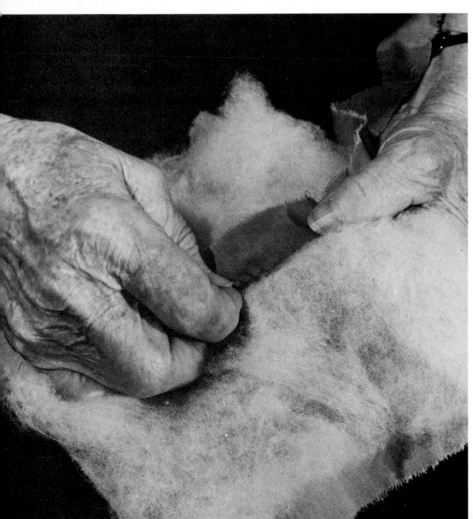

Attach a light color "log" to one edge of the center square by placing it face down and stitching through the filling and backing.

Using tiny scissors, cut the attached "log" the length of the center square.

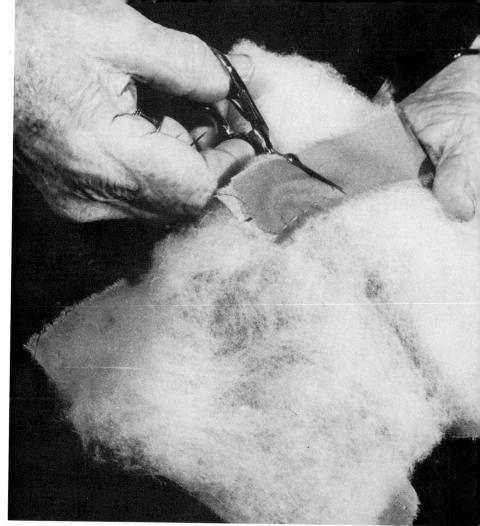

Working around the center square, add a second light color "log," stitching through the three thicknesses. Cut this "log" the length of the center square plus the first "log" width.

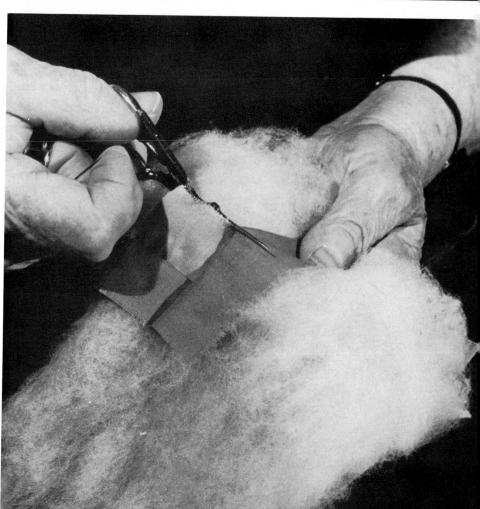

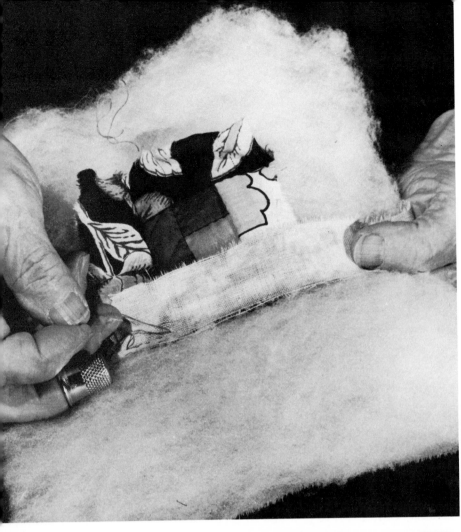

On the opposite two sides of the center square, add dark color "logs" and trim, squaring off each side. Continue "framing" the center square in light and dark colors, using both solids and prints, until you reach the edges of the 9-inch square of backing.

One completed block with both a light and a dark corner.

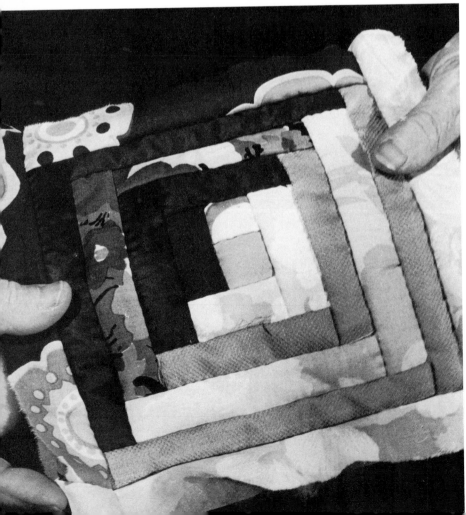

o join two completed blocks, place the sides with the same color effect together. When four blocks are joined, the design in the center will form either a dark or a light diamond. (It is best to complete all of your blocks before setting them together to be certain you have worked out your design properly.)

ttach two completed blocks by placing right sides together and stitching the connecting seam through the block top only. This can be done either by hand or by machine. Do not join all three layers.

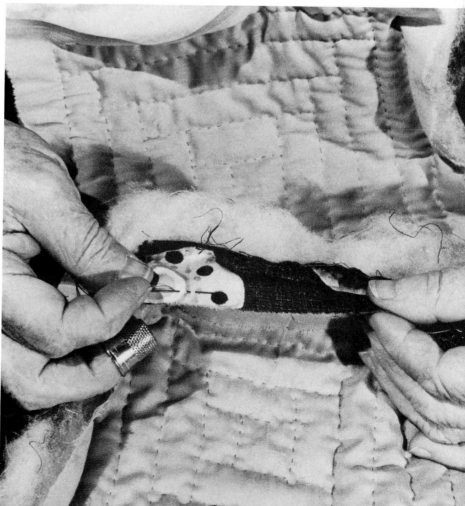

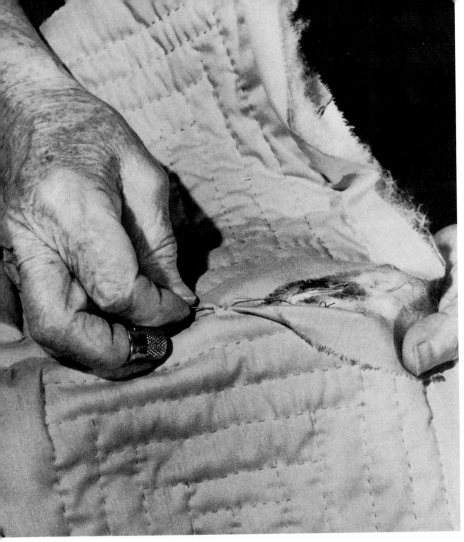

Turn the blocks over and seam the backing together by hand. Assemble all of the blocks in the same manner.

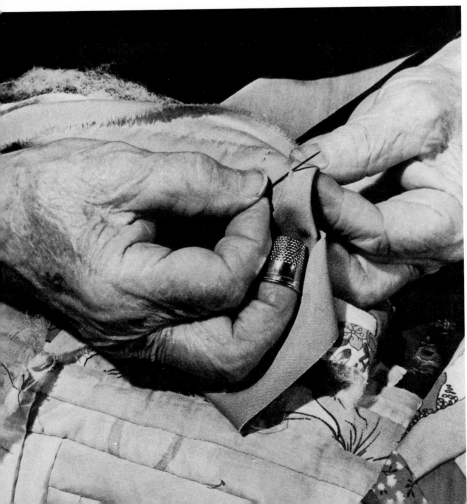

To bind the assembled quilt, use strips of material cut on the bias; stitch binding first to the quilt backing, then fold and whip to quilt top by hand.

allowances). Log lengths will be cut as each strip is attached to the block.

Follow the quilt-as-you-go steps illustrated in the photographs for making the *Log Cabin* "light and dark" pattern. Any pattern design may be easily adapted to this method of quilting.

As you can see, this particular pattern does not require a border, so that when you put the binding around the four sides, your quilt is finished — and beautiful.

Quilting on a Frame — To be certain that we had the last word on quilting on a frame, we went out to Pumpkin Center, Alabama, and spent the day with Mrs. W. A. Odom and her daughter, Mrs. Myrtle Stevens.

They just happened to be putting in a *Bear's Paw* design that day, and we watched them step-by-step, from the time they dropped the frame down from the ceiling, until the last stitch in the hem was put in.

These women are professionals. They have been quilting for the public for many years, and their quilts are flowering all over the United States. This mother-and-daughter team always quilts on a frame, and their frames are all made by their sons and brothers. About the largest quilt they can make on their frame is 90" x 108".

They do not use the "C" clamps that so many quilters use, preferring to use large nails which can be inserted into holes and pulled out as they roll their quilts. And since they keep the frame assembled at all times, they use a nylon cord to raise and lower it into place from the ceiling. The cord also anchors the frame in place, so there is no need to use the old-fashioned four-chair routine.

After assembling the quilt top and cutting the filling and backing fabrics to the correct size, follow the photographs as Mrs. Stevens demonstrates how to quilt on a frame.

TUFTING

Tufting (or tying) is a popular alternative to quilting stitches. It can be found in many old quilts, made when fillings were composed of such materials as fleece, leaves, newspapers, cornhusks, etc.

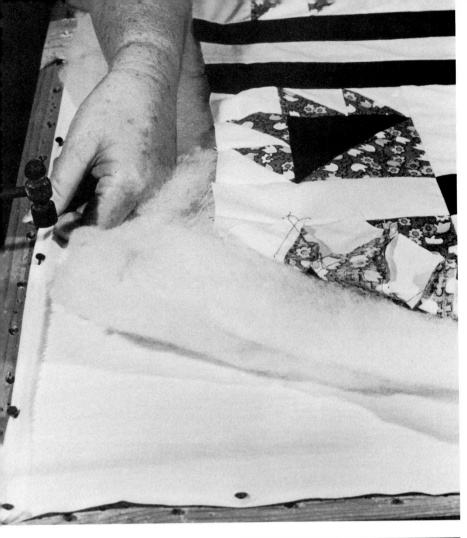

Tack the backing fabric to the frame.

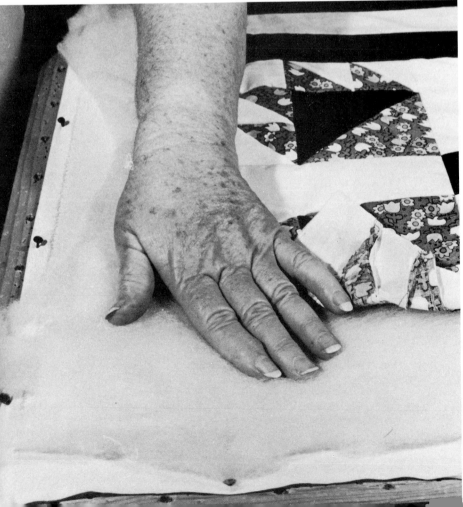

Smooth the filling over the taut backing, making sure it is not lumpy.

Place the quilt top on the filling and pin through the three layers on all four sides. Mark your quilting design on the quilt top if you do not plan on following the pattern lines. Mrs. Stevens uses a measured cord and tailor's chalk to draw her shell quilting design.

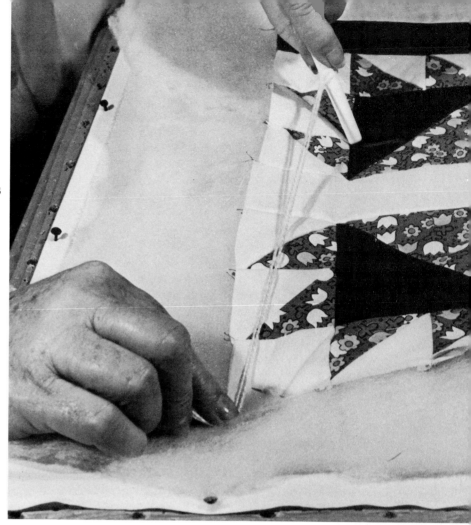

Following the chalk marks, quilt the design using small, even, running stitches through the three layers.

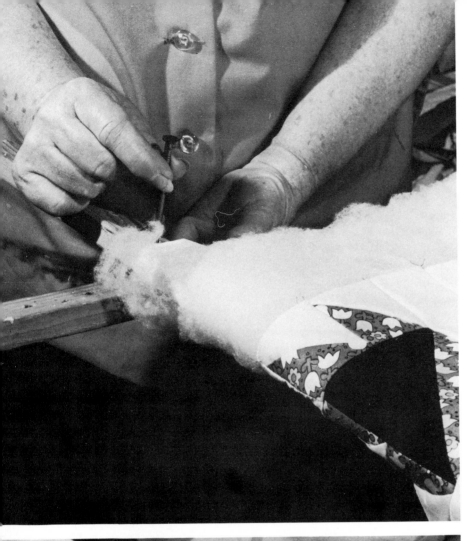

After quilting one complete side, remove the large nails from the two end corners of the frame and turn the frame rail, thereby rolling the quilt under. Replace the nails in a closer hole to secure the frame. In this manner, the center moves toward the frame edge where it is easily reached for quilting.

When all quilting is completed, remove the pins. Mrs. Stevens uses excess backing and filling to bind her quilt by turning it over the quilt top and whipping it down as you would any hem. Should you bind your quilt with separate strips of material, it is easiest first to remove the quilt entirely from the frame.

Two riotiously colorful examples of pieced quilts are these from the Steed collection. On the left, *Pineapple*, found among the patterns in this book; on the right, *Going Around the Mountain*.

In tufting, the three layers of the quilt are tied together with either matching or contrasting colors. This not only gives it a very puffy appearance, but the tufts add an interesting pattern of their own.

Usually, several layers of filling are used if a quilt is to be tufted. Mark the quilt top with pins or tailor's chalk. Be sure the points are evenly spaced and keep in mind that the closer the tufts, the stronger the quilt will be. Using a large needle and a double length of knitting worsted (many quilters prefer candlewick yarn for its strength), hold one end of the yarn while you push the needle through the quilt top to the backing and up again about ¼ inch away from where you began. Tie the two yarn ends securely in a double knot and cut ends to about ½ inch long.

Tufting is not as sturdy a method of completing a quilt as the traditional quilting stitches. Keep this in mind when you plan where your quilt is to be used.

Postscripts

 Many aspects of quilting have been passed over lightly, but enough of the basics are here to help even a beginner create her own treasure. And be sure to sign your quilt.

Miss Sallie Hill, who for many years was a foremost home department editor with *Progressive Farmer*, believes that "Inasmuch as so many of the heirloom quilts of the past were never fully identified because their makers never left any identifying marks, and it is really sad when you think about it, I think it behooves one who quilts to sign her quilt and date it, either where you can see it, or like an artist, tucked away in some corner. Because people are interested in identifying with the personality behind a quilt, they want to know who put in all those hours and created such a glorious thing of beauty."

Hundreds of women throughout the country responded to *Progressive Farmer*'s Quilt Block Contest, and here you will see sixty of the blocks and their patterns. Awards were given in two categories: traditional or old-time patterns, and modern or original patterns.

Judging for the contest was conducted by an independent panel, and entries were judged on quality of workmanship, use of color, fabric choice and combination, and overall appearance. The entries had to be all handstitched. Since the contest was for quilt blocks, it was not necessary for a woman to have ever made a quilt from her pattern.

As you examine the blocks and patterns and meet the women who made them, in many instances you may say: "Well, she didn't tell me how many blocks I would need, and she didn't give me the yardage." The reasons she didn't are simple. In many instances, there simply has never been a quilt made from the pattern. But each pattern tells the size and directions for making one block, so it's easy for you to estimate the number of blocks needed for the size quilt you desire.

A number of entries incorporated bits and pieces of living history: scraps from a wedding dress, pieces from a son's bride's dress, appliquéd cutouts from some heirloom English chintz, a butterfly from ... well, who knows, but it had a special meaning for that particular woman.

Unfortunately, of the two hundred women who received honorable mention awards, only a few could be among "The Love Patches." The blocks that were selected were chosen on the basis of their patterns. We wanted to give you a cross-section of those patterns that most nearly represent the patchwork patterns from days long past and original designs that are sure to become just as enduring.

You will see classics such as *Delectable Mountains* and *Blazing Star*. You will see poignant reminders of the past in *Balloon Girl*, an appliqué with delicate embroidery. And you will see exciting new designs such as *Oriental Bouquets*.

Each pattern is a love patch, and we just wish this book could include all the entries, for every one of them, whether pieced or appliquéd, is patched with love.

The Love Patches

Grandma's Square

Mrs. C. C. Venable
England, Arkansas

You may have wondered where the name of this chapter originated. Mrs. Venable inspired "The Love Patches," for no one better exemplifies what quilts are all about — love.

From the time Mrs. Venable's *Grandma's Square* pattern was announced as one of the winners in the quilt block contest, she has been surrounded by women clamoring for her wonderful design, and she has answered every one of them with a love-patched square. Now, *Grandma's Square* belongs to the ages, for no one need seek farther than these pages.

Each piece measures 1 inch square (plus seam allowances). One 17-inch square block requires 289 tiny squares. If 30 such blocks are set 5 across and 6 down, with a 2½-inch border, the finished quilt should measure 90″ x 107″.

Mrs. Venable's creation is particularly interesting, not only because she used so many different fabrics, but because she worked her colors so effectively in rows of light to medium to dark. By alternating her tiny squares of color, Mrs. Venable created a diamond-shaped design within each 17-inch square block.

For one block you will need:
  289 squares — prints and solids
    (the center square should be
    different from all other fabrics
    used)
Allow ¼ inch for seams on all
pattern pieces.

Double Wreath

Mrs. O. W. Smith

Lepanto, Arkansas

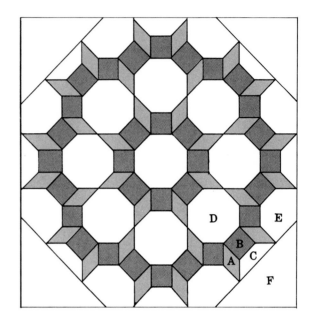

Mrs. Smith wrote that she was more than happy to share the pattern for *Double Wreath* with other women who enjoy quilting. Her directions are simple but clear:

Twenty 20-inch square blocks (plus seam allowances) make a beautiful quilt. Mrs. Smith set her blocks together with 3-inch strips and suggests finishing the quilt with a 3-inch border. When set 4 across and 5 down, the quilt should measure approximately 95″ x 118″.

For one block you will need:
   A — 32 red diamonds
   B — 32 blue squares
   C — 8 white pieces
   D — 9 white octagons
   E — 8 white pieces
   F — 4 white triangles
Each pattern piece includes a ¼-inch seam allowance.

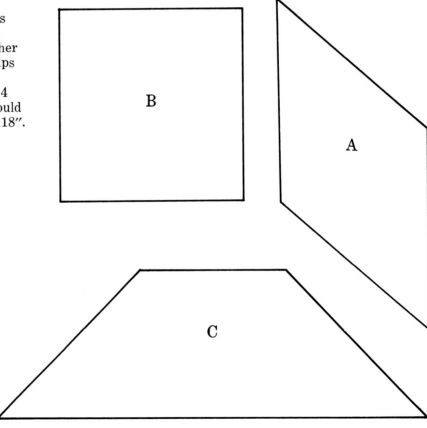

70

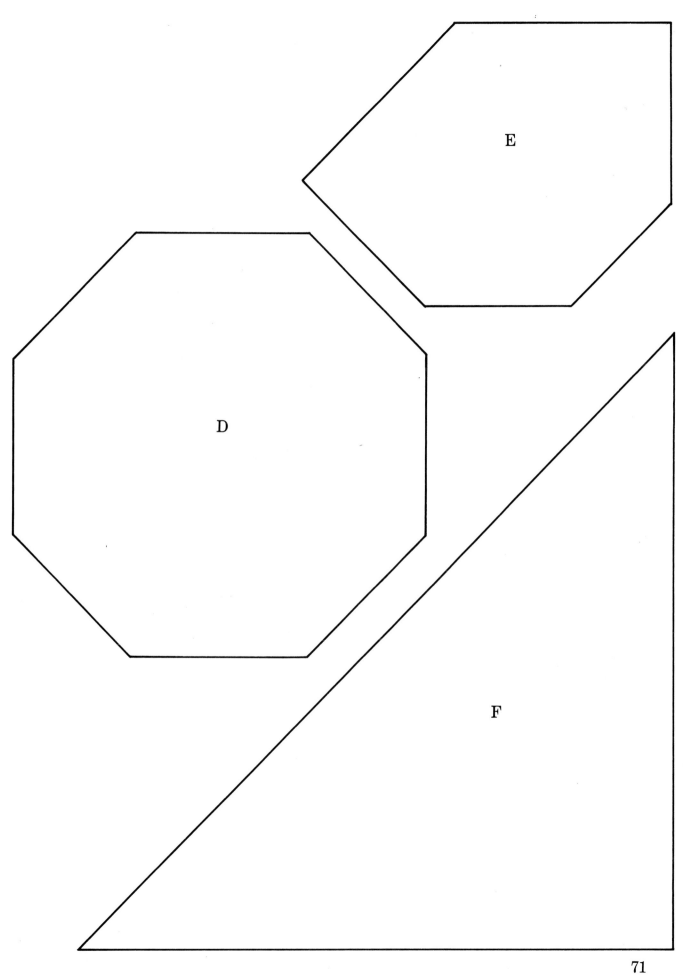

D

E

F

President's Wreath

Mrs. Annie Linder
Eastview, Kentucky

Apparently many people shared the judges' enthusiasm for Mrs. Linder's stunning quilt pattern, for she has been making *President's Wreath* quilts ever since the winners' list was published.

"This pattern was taken from a very old quilt," she wrote. "At the time, I did not know the name of it, but later saw it in a magazine with a group of other quilts and it had the name *President's Wreath*.

Mrs. Linder appliqués her wreath on a block of white material 22 inches square (plus seam allowances). With 12 blocks set 3 across and 4 down with 3-inch strips between each block, the quilt will measure 72″ x 97″. A border will make the quilt larger.

Mrs. Linder repeats the flowers and leaves of the pattern for her quilting design. The overall effect is truly fit for a president.

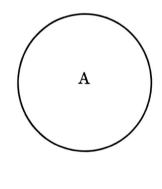

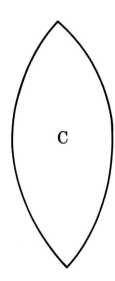

For one block you will need:
  A — 4 yellow print centers
  B — 4 green print stems
  C — 24 green print leaves
  D — 4 red print flowers
  E — 8 red print buds
  F — 8 green print pieces
Allow ¼ inch for seams on all pattern pieces.

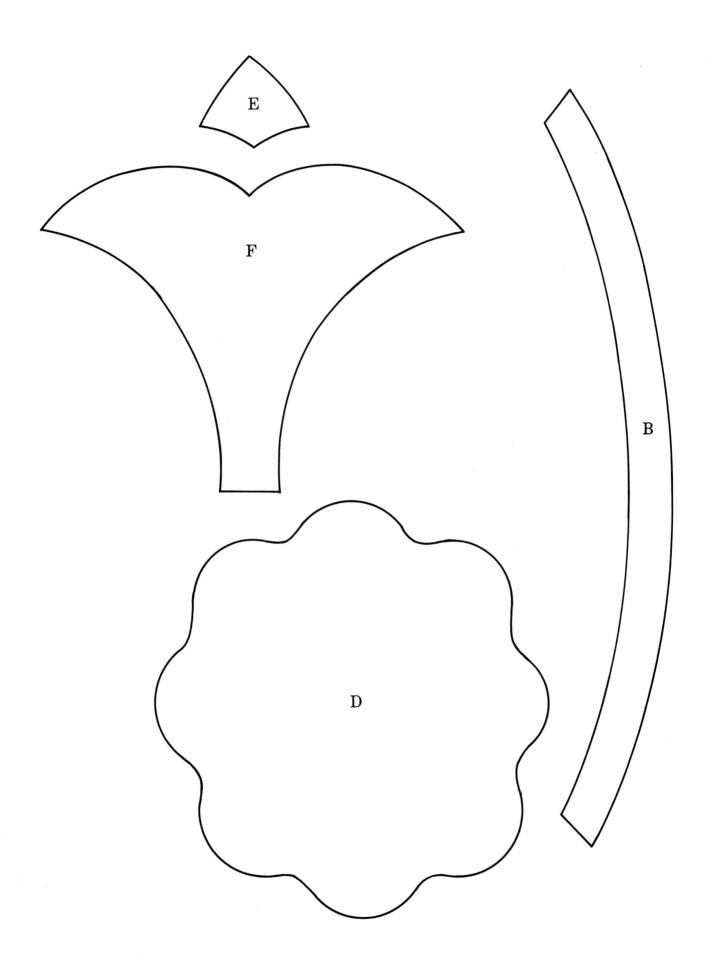

E

F

B

D

73

Oriental Bouquets

Mrs. Dorsey Zalants
Columbia, South Carolina

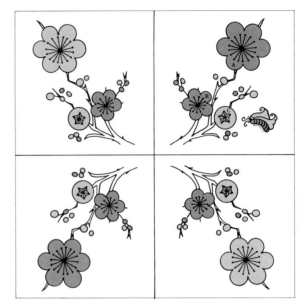

We knew we would be beleaguered by women wanting to know everything about Mrs. Zalants's magnificent original pattern, so we decided to let this mistress of the drawing board and needle tell you about *Oriental Bouquets.*

"I got the idea for the design," Mrs. Zalants wrote, "from a Chinese hawthorn jar. And I just took it from there. I used all cotton and polyester material and thread (everything is washable)."

Mrs. Zalants worked all the embroidery before appliquéing the large flowers. She embroidered the stems of the flowers in the coral stitch, using a double (2 strands) of DMC No. 3 embroidery thread, and worked all the small flowers in the satin stitch, using DMC No. 3 for some and DMC No. 25 for the rest.

Mrs. Zalants cut paper patterns for flowers A, B, and C to use for cutting the polyester filling and the appliqué fabric. She basted the polyester filling loosely to the fabric, basted the appliqué fabric over the filling, and worked it to the fabric using a close buttonhole stitch.

To give the quilt an "at random" look, Mrs. Zalants did not put the butterfly in every block but scattered it around.

Allow 1/4 inch for seams on all pattern pieces.

74

75

Grandmother's Pieced Tulip

Mrs. Irene Goodrich
Columbus, Ohio

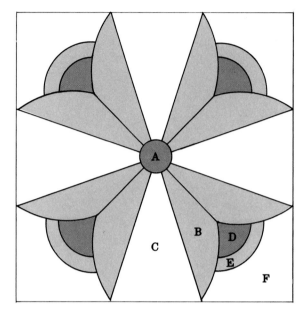

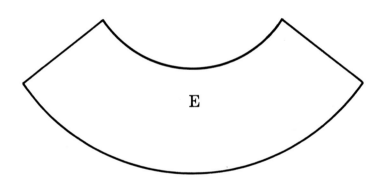

According to Mrs. Goodrich, this pattern should not be attempted by a beginning quilter, and she should know — she has been working on quilt patches since she was 4 years old! Currently, she is making each of her nineteen nieces and nephews a quilt, three of which are completed and in use, and three more in various stages of creation.

In addition to her quilting library, Mrs. Goodrich has three quilting frames: an oval, a massive old antique, and a modern one. She also has quilt pen pals and they have a lot of fun writing to each other and exchanging ideas and quilt items.

A nice size quilt will require 32 pieced blocks and 31 plain. A finished block measures approximately 10 inches square (plus seam allowances). The 31 plain blocks will take 3¼ yards of 36-inch solid material (Mrs. Goodrich used unbleached muslin), and the backing will require 5 yards of solid material. By arranging the 63 blocks with 7 across and 9 down, the quilt will measure 70" x 90".

For one block you will need:
A — 1 green circle
B — 8 rose pieces
C — 4 white triangles
D — 4 print pieces
E — 4 light pieces
F — 4 white pieces
Each pattern piece includes a
¼-inch seam allowance.

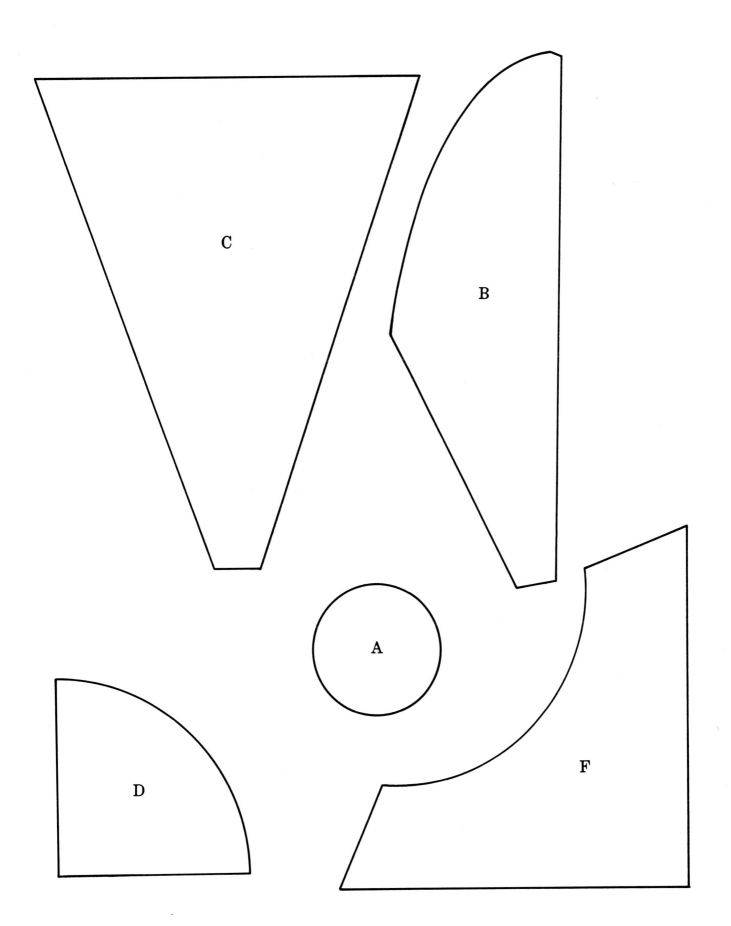

Green Pastures

Beatrice Gladys Baker
Zebulon, North Carolina

Miss Baker's exciting original appliqué pattern captured the heart and eye of every beholder, and the judges had no problem awarding her a prize for inspired originality.

The possibilities for animals in Miss Baker's design are almost limitless — horses, cows, sheep, goats, birds, butterflies, grasshoppers. They may be embroidered, appliquéd, painted, or done in a combination of these techniques.

Color possibilities, too, are limitless. Why not a *Green Pastures* in blue, or purple, or pink? A flower print replacing the green could make *Flowering Meadows,* an adaptation of *Green Pastures.*

Seams should be carefully pressed before pieces are joined. Seams of the flowered strip should be pressed toward the center of the strip. Seams of the fence rails should be pressed toward the center of the rails. Seams of the fence posts should be pressed toward the center of the posts, including the one at the top but not the one at the bottom.

Quilting should be done outside and close to the flower strip, fence rails, and fence posts, except at the bottom of the posts. This makes these pieces stand out, and the posts look as though their bottoms are hidden in the flowers. The seam

joining the pasture to the fence assembly is not quilted, thus becoming less conspicuous.

With twelve 18-inch square blocks (plus seam allowances), set 3 across and 4 down, and a harmonizing 12-inch border, the quilt will measure about 78″ x 96″. The fence and a few birds or butterflies could be quilted into the border.

For one block you will need:
A — 2 birds
B — 1 horse
Strips—1 charcoal 2½″ x 18½″
    1 flowered 2½″ x 18½″
    3 brown posts 1¼″ x
     4¼″
    4 brown rails 1¼″ x
     3⅛″
    4 brown rails 1¼″ x
     5¾″
    6 green strips 1¼″ x
     3⅛″
    6 green strips 1½″ x
     5¾″
    1 green strip 10¾″ x
     18½″
Each pattern piece includes a
¼-inch seam allowance.

National Star

Gertrude Mitchell
Russell Springs, Kentucky

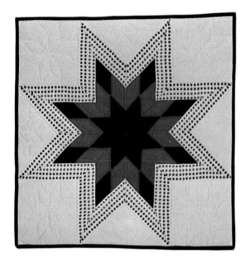

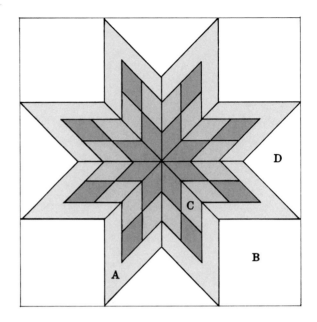

National Star — a veritable star of a pattern — is an original, and Mrs. Mitchell wrote that she regretted not being able to give the exact measurements for a quilt. She simply made the block for the contest, and she has had many people begging her to make a quilt for them. If you could see the original pieced block, you would understand why. The quilting on the white background is a smaller version of the same star, and it is delicately beautiful. Some shining star — that Mrs. Mitchell!

Each block measures approximately 10½ inches square.

For one block you will need:
A — 16 print pieces
B — 4 white squares
C — 32 solid diamonds (16 red, 16 blue)
D — 4 white triangles
Each pattern piece includes a ¼-inch seam allowance.

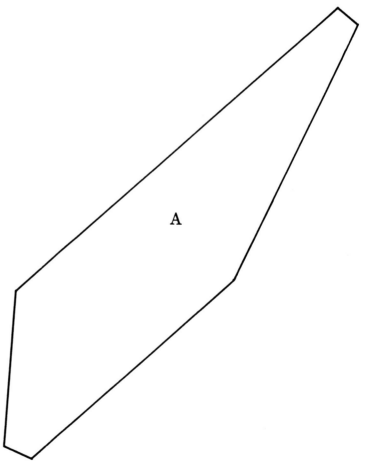

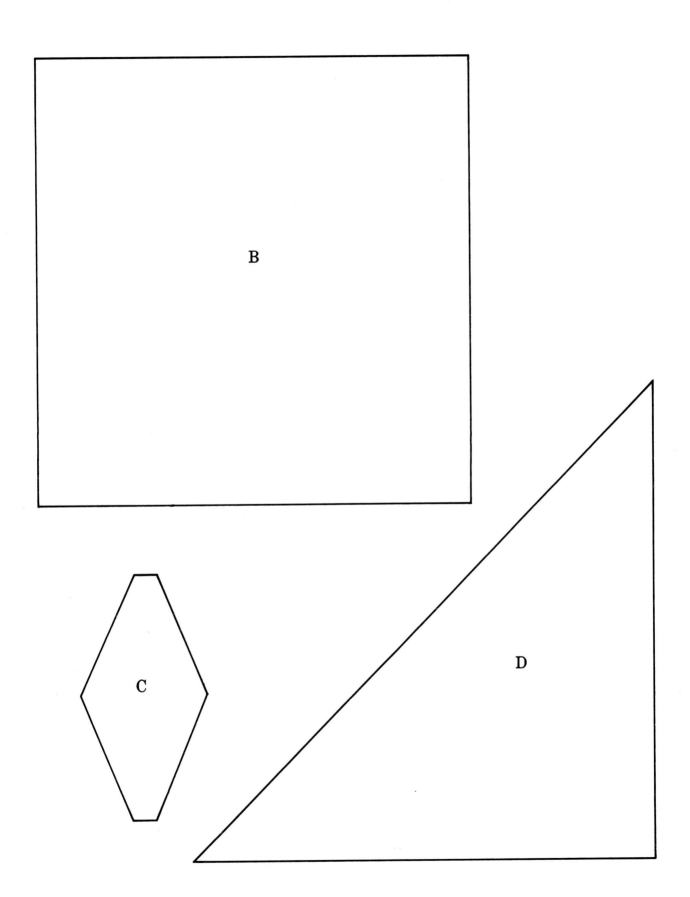

The Strawberry

Izola B. Marple
Buchannon, West Virginia

"I designed and made a quilt like this in 1971," wrote Mrs. Marple when she sent in the pattern for her outstanding appliqué pattern. "I designed the quilting pattern, too, and made it to exhibit in the Arts and Crafts Exhibit at the Strawberry Festival, which is held in June every year in Buchannon. I won the first-place ribbon in the appliqué division."

If you could see the actual quilt block that Mrs. Marple entered, you would not have to look twice to know why she is a winner. *The Strawberry* looks good enough to eat — and we hope you'll get into the act and make yourself this delight.

Mrs. Marple used 14-inch square white blocks (plus seam allowances). She cut a red strawberry and a green cap for each appliqué. Make sure the petal cap overlaps the strawberry as shown in the pattern.

If 30 blocks are set together with 4-inch strips of red material, 5 across and 6 down, and finished with a 2-inch border, the completed quilt should measure 90″ x 108″.

As a gorgeous finishing touch, Mrs. Marple embroidered tiny gold French knots as the strawberry seeds. She suggests quilting diagonally ¾ inch apart. Do not quilt through the strawberry. When the quilt is finished, turn and quilt through backing and filling only behind each appliqué.

Allow ¼ inch for seams on all pattern pieces.

Grandma's Zinnia Basket

Ruby Magness

Dermott, Arkansas

This exciting appliqué pattern is an original, and when word of it got around, Mrs. Magness had people writing her from five states! It has been in Mrs. Magness's family for over a hundred years, so you can see that it is as traditional as can be, and yet as modern as tomorrow.

Cut twelve 24-inch square blocks (plus seam allowances). Draw the basket outline. Have bottom of basket about 2 inches above edge of material. Draw diagonal lines about 1 inch apart across the basket and 2 horizontal lines across the "neck" of the basket. The basket strips are cut on the bias 1 inch wide. Fold the edges to the center to make each strip ½ inch wide; baste on penciled diagonal lines. Then double fold 2 strips to make them ¼ inch wide to cross the "neck" of the basket.

Next, baste ½-inch-wide bias strips on the sides and bottom of the basket outline. Baste the flower stems and leaves touching the top of the basket. (Stem lengths may vary according to your desires.) Now cover the ends with a ½-inch-wide bias strip on the top of the basket. Pin the flowers in place so you can arrange the stems and leaves, and baste. Then you're ready to start whipping them down.

Mrs. Magness makes all 72 flowers before starting anything else, and she uses 3 different color combinations: 12 of one color, 24 of another, and 36 of the third.

Take the 2½-inch-wide strip of material that is your flower (length depends upon how full you wish your flowers to be) and gather one long side of it up close (this is the side that will be under the flower's center). On the opposite long side, turn the seam under; sew it by hand using zigzag stitches; gather. This will give the appearance of a solid flower and its petals. Then sew the two short ends together.

Mrs. Magness assembled her 12 blocks 3 across and 4 down with 4-inch strips between each block and a 4-inch border all the way around. This gives her a quilt approximately 88″ x 116″.

For one block you will need:
- A — 16 strips (4 for basket outline, 10 diagonal lines, 2 horizontal lines)
- B — 6 circles for flower centers
- C — 6 large leaves
- D — 21 small leaves
- E — 3 stems
- F — 6 flowers

Allow ¼ inch for seams on all pattern pieces.

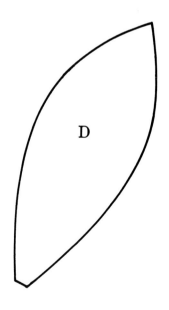

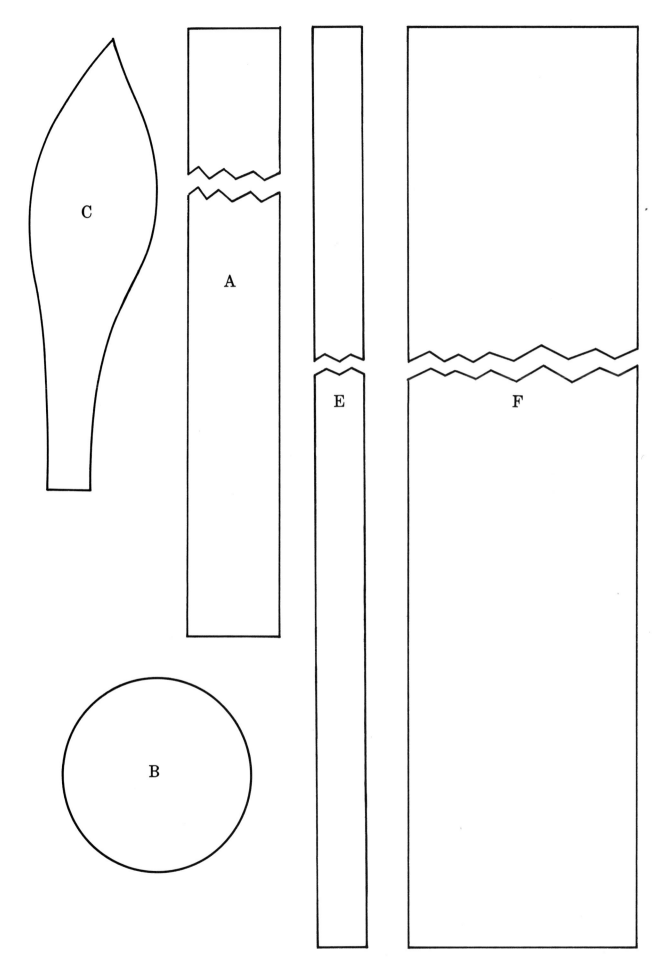

C

A

B

E

F

85

Bride's Quilt

Bessie C. Bowman
Boones Mill, Virginia

This is one of two quilt patterns Mrs. Bowman submitted to the quilt block contest. Under the category of traditional or old-time patterns, she said that the first time she saw the *Bride's Quilt* pattern was in *Progressive Farmer* about eight years ago.

Mrs. Bowman said the pattern was taken from an original in a New York museum, and dates back to the 1880s. She liked it so well that she made one, and today it complements her four-poster bed.

Mrs. Bowman appliquéd twenty 16-inch square blocks (plus seam allowances). She assembled her quilt using 4 blocks across and 5 blocks down with a 4-inch strip between each block. The finished quilt measures approximately 76″ x 96″. The pattern lends itself beautifully to a border of hearts which would make the quilt larger.

For one block you will need:
  A — 27 leaves (9 yellow, 10 green, 8 red)
  B — 8 hearts (4 green, 4 red)
  Circular stem — ½-inch wide dark brown strip
Allow ¼ inch for seams on all pattern pieces.

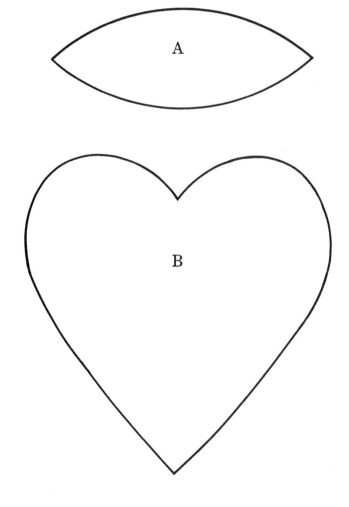

Tulip

Edith S. Longmire
Andersonville, Tennessee

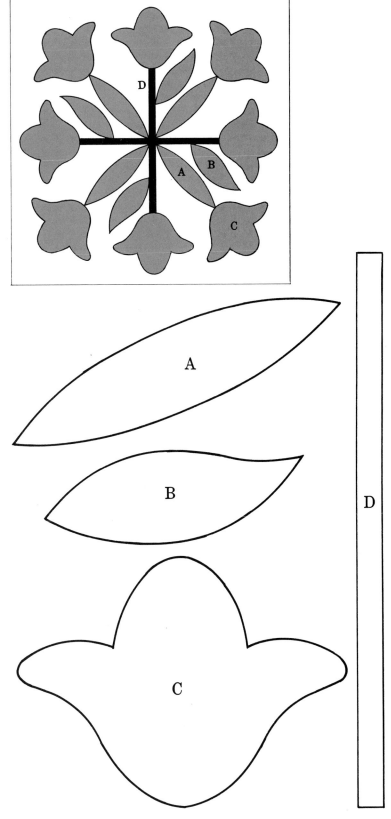

This traditional old-timer showed up so beautifully among the quilt blocks that we simply had to include it in the sixty patterns. Just to look at it makes you think spring will be in bloom all year long. The pattern is so outstanding that it can be used with any decor.

Mrs. Longmire's finished block measures about 12 inches square. On a white background, almost any combination of bright colors would be gorgeous. Hasn't it been said that any color is welcome in a garden?

Her pattern is a bright appliqué: 2 tulips in lavender, 2 in strawberry pink, 2 in pink and yellow print, 2 in an old-fashioned floral print, and stem and leaves in dark green.

The blocks may be set together with a strip of any of the materials, and then a border may be made of the same material. When quilted, the tulips appear three-dimensional.

For one block you will need:
A — 4 dark green leaves
B — 4 dark green leaves
C — 8 tulips (4 solid, 4 print)
D — 2 dark green stems
Allow ¼ inch for seams on all pattern pieces.

87

Democrat Banner

Mary A. Cole
Columbia, Kentucky

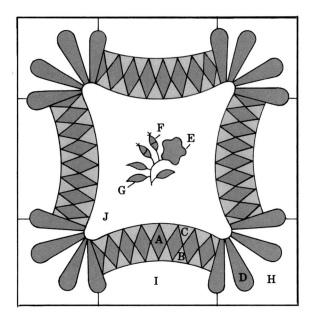

The original quilt designed from this pattern was made in 1881 by the Todd sisters, and was shown at the first Adair County Fair in Columbia, Kentucky. Mary Cole wrote, "As far as I know, this quilt pattern has never been copied. The quilt has taken many blue ribbons since the first showing. I am a grandneice of the makers and will pass it on to the next in line."

Her quilt pattern, with its outstanding design and border, should become an all-American classic.

The blocks are approximately 20 inches square (plus seam allowances). An 84" x 110" quilt has 3 blocks across and 4 blocks down, with 6-inch strips between each block and a 6-inch border.

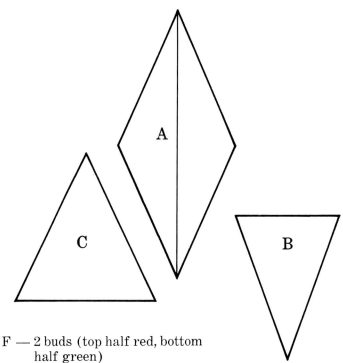

For one block you will need:
- A — 32 print diamonds (4 cut in half lengthwise)
- B — 32 red triangles
- C — 32 red triangles
- D — 16 green pieces
- E — 1 red rose (the stem is a narrow strip of fabric cut on the bias)
- F — 2 buds (top half red, bottom half green)
- G — 3 green leaves
- H — 4 white pieces
- I — 4 white pieces (dotted line indicates fold)
- J — 1 white piece (pattern reduced — dotted line indicates fold and should measure 8¾ inches long)

Allow ¼ inch for seams on all pattern pieces.

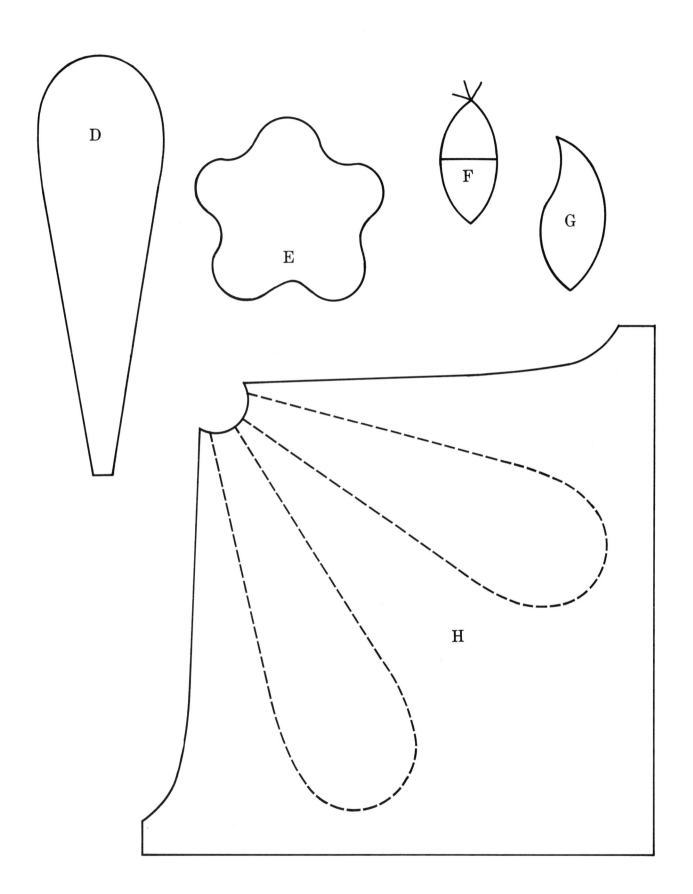

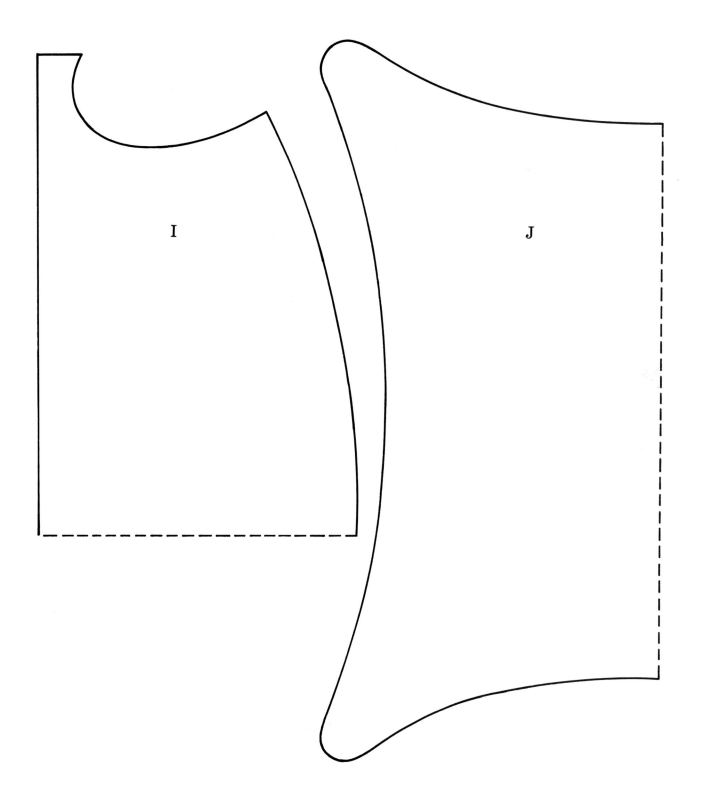

I

J

Wreath

Mrs. Russell A. Warehime
Westminster, Maryland

Mrs. Warehime's pattern is a very old one. "The pattern has been handed down from my mother, who quilted quite a few of them," Mrs. Warehime wrote.

Wreath took a first prize and special award last year at the Maryland State Fair, and if you could actually see it, you'd understand why. Mrs. Warehime loves to quilt, and she goes to her county Farm Museum and helps the Homemaker's Club with its quilting every chance she gets.

Mrs. Warehime's pattern is magnificent with 26 different shades of colors for the design and an intricate floral pattern quilted in the center.

Each block measures 18 inches square (plus seam allowances), and the wreath circle within the block is about 11¾ inches in diameter. Each wreath has 26 leaves and 2 rows of embroidery for the vine and individual leaf stems.

After attaching the completed blocks, Mrs. Warehime finished her quilt by making a 9-inch border with a double running vine of green leaves. With 20 blocks set 4 across and 5 down plus the border dimensions, your quilt will be approximately 90″ x 108″.

Allow ¼ inch for seams on all pattern pieces.

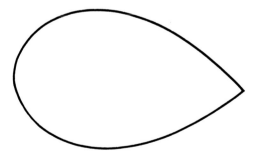

91

Cathedral Windows

Nancy Howard
Ravenna, Kentucky

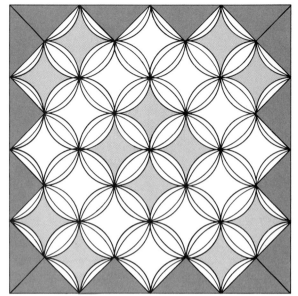

Mrs. Howard's gorgeous quilt block was chosen from a large field of similar patterns because its size was such that design intricacies could be more easily seen by a beginning quilter.

You may find this pattern under varying names such as *Stained-Glass Windows, Double Wedding Ring,* or *Attic Windows.* Yet whatever it is called, *Cathedral Windows* has appeared in many publications not only because it is a beautiful pattern but because it is one of the most difficult pieced designs to execute.

It requires no filling, quilting stitches, or even a separate backing. Each piece is folded in such a way that the completed square appears to have all three quilt layers and to have been quilted. Magic? Yes, and Mrs. Howard's creation is stunning in blue, white, and a blue, pink, and white print.

There are several ways of making this complicated pattern. The method given here is slightly less complicated than others for it requires fewer stitches. Be sure your measurements are exact.

Begin with one 6-inch square piece of solid material (this includes seam allowance). Find the exact center by folding the square diagonally in both directions. Mark the center with a tiny pencil dot. Press in the 1/4-inch seam

allowances on all four sides. Fold each corner to the center point and press flat. Again, fold the four corners to the center, pin, and press flat. (If your material is not perfectly square to begin with, your corner folds will not fit together.) Stitch the corner points together in the center through all folded layers. The folded fabric now measures 2¾ inches square.

One quilt block requires 16 folded squares. After completing all 16, attach them by placing right sides together and slip-stitching the edges with matching thread. The assembled quilt block should measure 11 inches square.

Cut the 1½-inch square "window" patches. Arranging the print and white patches to your liking, set them over the seam lines in the small squares formed by two adjoining 2¾-inch squares (see diagram). Now fold one edge (it will appear curved when folded) of the "window" square over the "window" fabric and slip-stitch into place. Continue doing this on each side of all 24 "windows" in the block.

Fifty-six 11-inch blocks set 7 across and 8 down will make a quilt 77" x 88". The quilt will have only half-squares at the edges. You may cut half-"windows" to fit or leave the edges solid, giving your pattern a built-in border.

For one block you will need:
   A — 24 "window" squares (12
       print, 12 white)
   B — 16 large solid squares
       (dotted lines indicate folds)
Pattern piece (B) includes a ¼-inch
seam allowance.

A

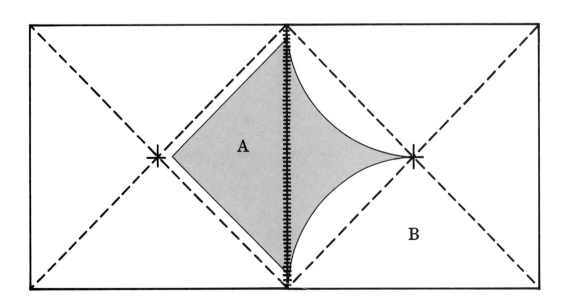

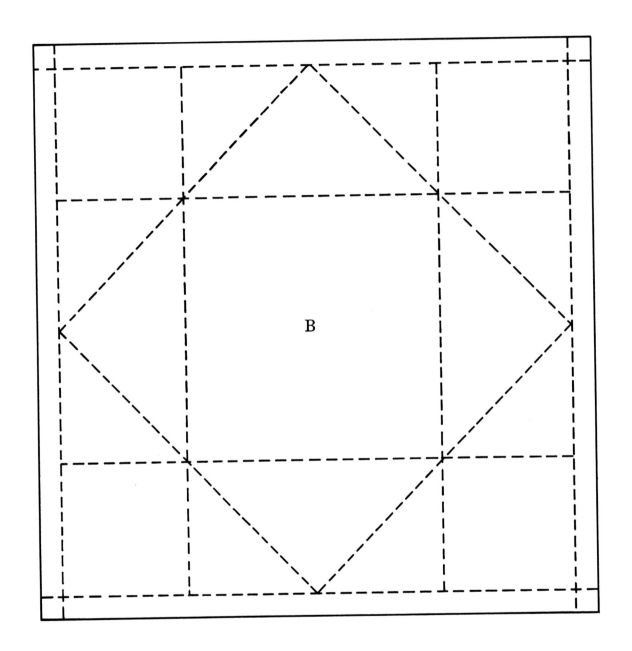

B

A Bit of Spring

Oda May Webb

St. David, Arizona

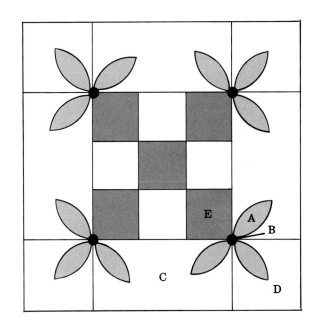

"**E**xhibiting at the county and state fairs has been my hobby for the past 25 years," Oda May wrote. "I love to do needlework and découpage, and I usually make at least one quilt a year to exhibit. There are certainly a lot of beautiful quilts on display at the fairs.

"My mother taught me to do all these things, such as quilting and needlework, when I was very young. I also do a lot of home canning, preserving, and jelly making."

Oda May's design is an original, and she apologized for having misplaced her original measurements. However, the use of 4 different prints against a solid white background should give anyone a lift, and since a finished block measures 10 inches square, it's easy to figure how many you would need to make a quilt of any size. When quilted, the petals appear three-dimensional.

For one block you will need:
- A — 12 print petals
- B — 4 print circles
- C — 4 solid rectangles (includes area of squares D and E)
- D — 4 solid squares (includes area of square E)
- E — 9 squares (5 print, 4 solid)

Allow ¼ inch for seams on all pattern pieces.

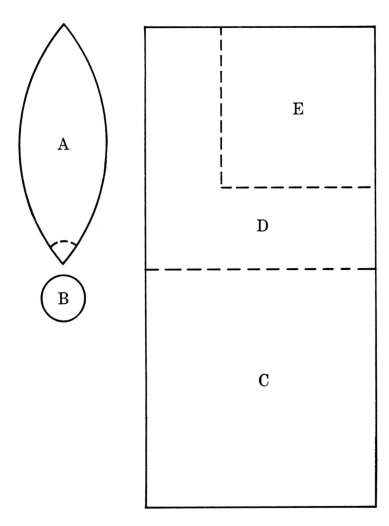

Flower Basket

Mrs. Nova Lowe
Hayesville, North Carolina

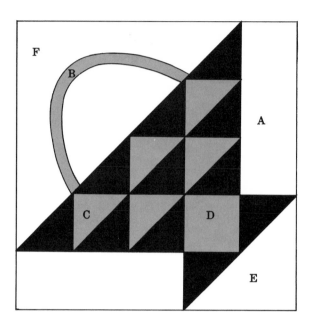

Mrs. Lowe chose a soft shade of orange for her *Flower Basket* and she brought it to its blooming glory with a contrasting floral print in orange, white, red, and black.

This pattern requires only half of the quilt blocks to be pieced. It is put together by alternating white squares, set on the diagonal, and it is filled in at the 4 sides of the quilt with white half-blocks.

Colonial in origin, the quilt will require 25 pieced blocks and 16 plain, each approximately 12 inches square (plus seam allowances) with 16 plain half-blocks set on the diagonal for the sides, and 4 plain ¼ blocks set on the diagonal for the corners. If you assemble your quilt in this manner, you will need about 6 yards of white material and 3½ yards of print.

Mrs. Lowe used a combination of diagonal and floral vine for her quilting pattern.

For one block you will need:
- A — 2 white rectangles
- B — 1 solid piece
- C — 16 triangles (11 prints, 5 white)
- D — 1 white square
- E — 1 white triangle
- F — 1 white triangle (pattern reduced — sides should equal 9½″ x 9½″ x 13½″)

Allow ¼ inch for seams on all pattern pieces.

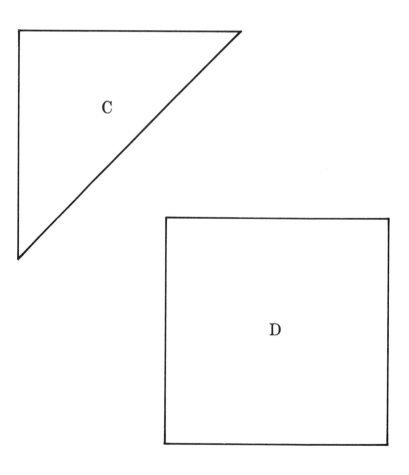

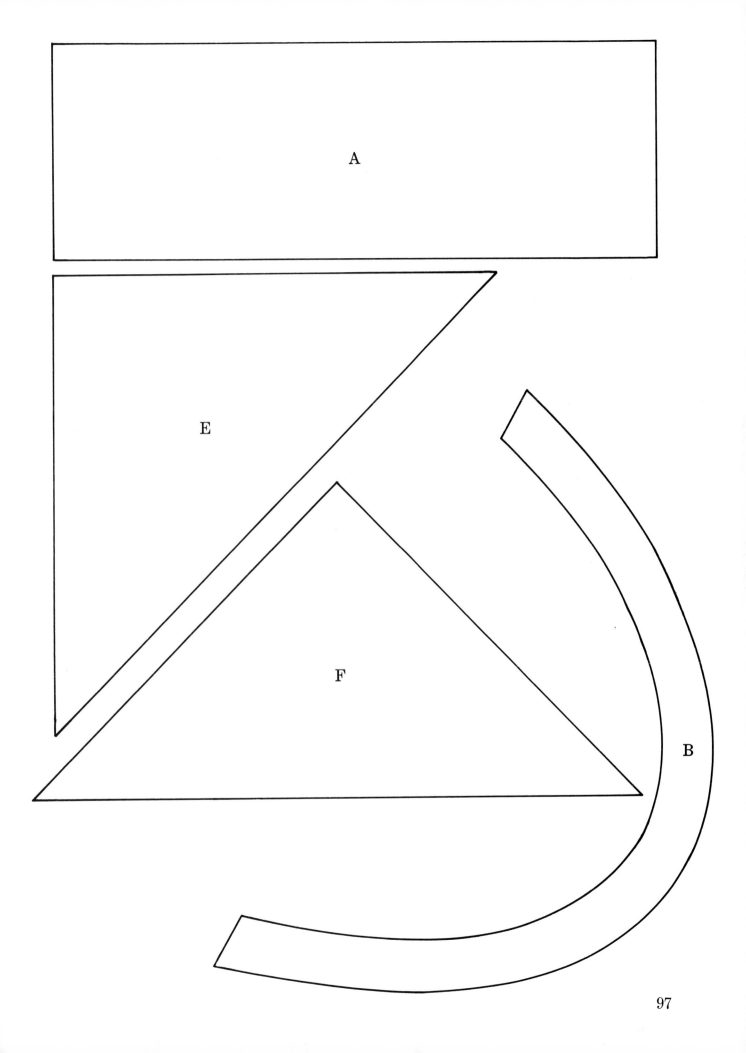

A

E

F

B

97

Martha Washington's Log Cabin

Mrs. Tom Yarbrough
Maysville, Georgia

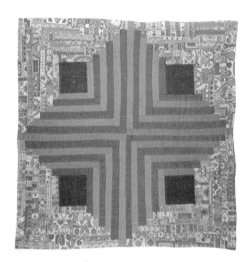

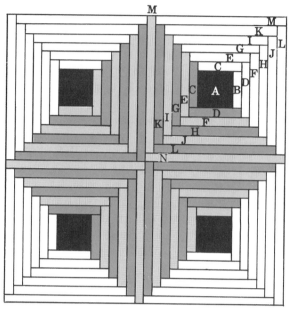

Bessie B. Yarbrough chose a traditional pattern for her entry, and it is one of the most attractive ones we've seen. For one thing, it has six "logs" on each side, as opposed to the usual five, and she said that when she first made this particular pattern, she had her "mamma's" quilt to go by. By now, however, she's made so many, it's as easy as, well, falling off a log.

Mrs. Yarbrough has made many beautiful quilts, and she said that years ago, when she paid 10 and 15 cents a yard for material, she could better afford to make them. Bessie said she stays busy as she sews for the public. Looking at this exciting and different *Log Cabin*, one can only conclude that she could stay busy just making this pattern.

To simplify the directions, each log is 1 inch wide and the center is 3 inches square. (Log lengths are given below.) Each log block measures 15 inches and 4 of these blocks pieced together create a light and dark diamond motif in 30-inch square blocks (plus seam allowances). If you set 9 such blocks 3 across and 3 down, your finished quilt would measure 90" x 90".

Beginning at the right of the center square and working counterclockwise, attach strips B through N in the sequence indicated in the above diagram until each side has 6 logs. To obtain the diamond motif Mrs. Yarbrough created so beautifully, work one corner (2 adjacent sides of the center square) in light fabrics and the opposite corner in dark fabrics. This pattern is particularly well suited for the quilt-as-you-go method described in the how-to chapter.

For one block you will need:
A — 1 center square
B — 1 log — 3 inches long
C — 2 logs — 4 inches long
D — 2 logs — 5 inches long
E — 2 logs — 6 inches long
F — 2 logs — 7 inches long
G — 2 logs — 8 inches long
H — 2 logs — 9 inches long
I — 2 logs — 10 inches long
J — 2 logs — 11 inches long
K — 2 logs — 12 inches long
L — 2 logs — 13 inches long
M — 2 logs — 14 inches long
N — 1 log — 15 inches long
Allow ¼ inch for seams on all pattern pieces.

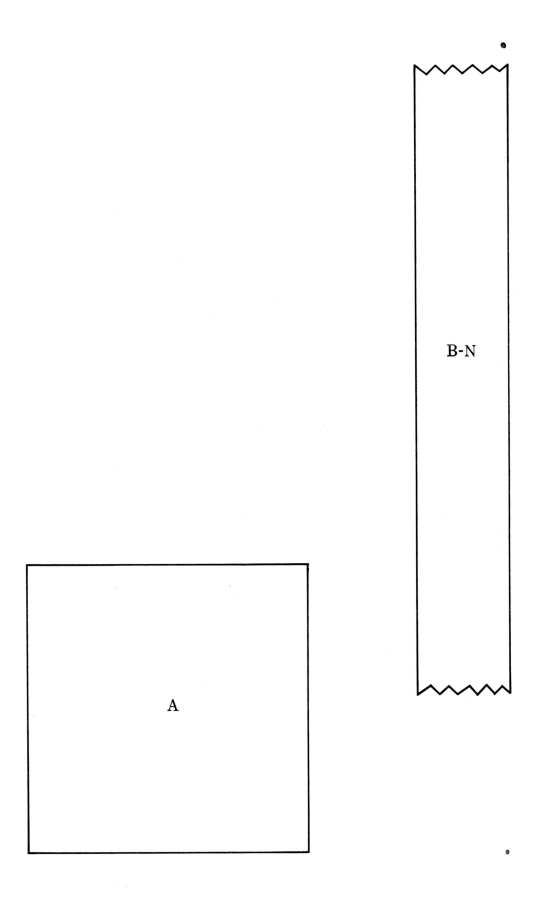

A

B-N

Appliqué Orchid Flower

Estella Cameron
Vinita, Oklahoma

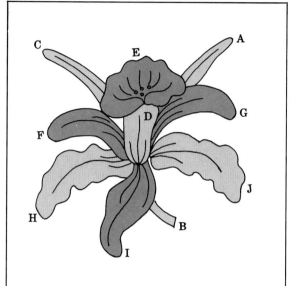

Perhaps, upon seeing this, you will think it should be growing in a greenhouse. Not on your life! This beautiful appliqué pattern could make your house a showplace, and Mrs. Cameron has written that she is very happy to share it with you.

In addition to the overall exquisiteness of her flower, Estella Cameron has embroidered each of the petals and leaves, and the quilting pattern, which is a series of four connecting curved feathers, is done in pink. The appliquéd flower is also quilted in an outline of pink.

For her orchid quilt, Mrs. Cameron suggested using 12 blocks 18 inches square (plus seam allowances). She sets the blocks together 3 across and 4 down with 6-inch strips between each block. If you add a matching border of 12 inches, the finished quilt will measure approximately 90″ x 114″.

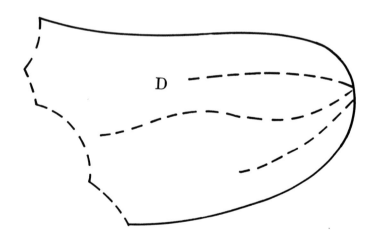

For one block you will need:
- A — 1 green leaf
- B — 1 green stem
- C — 1 green leaf
- D — 1 purple piece
- E — 1 lavender piece with yellow embroidery
- F — 1 lavender petal
- G — 1 pink petal
- H — 1 pink petal
- I — 1 purple petal
- J — 1 lavender petal

Allow ¼ inch for seams on all pattern pieces.

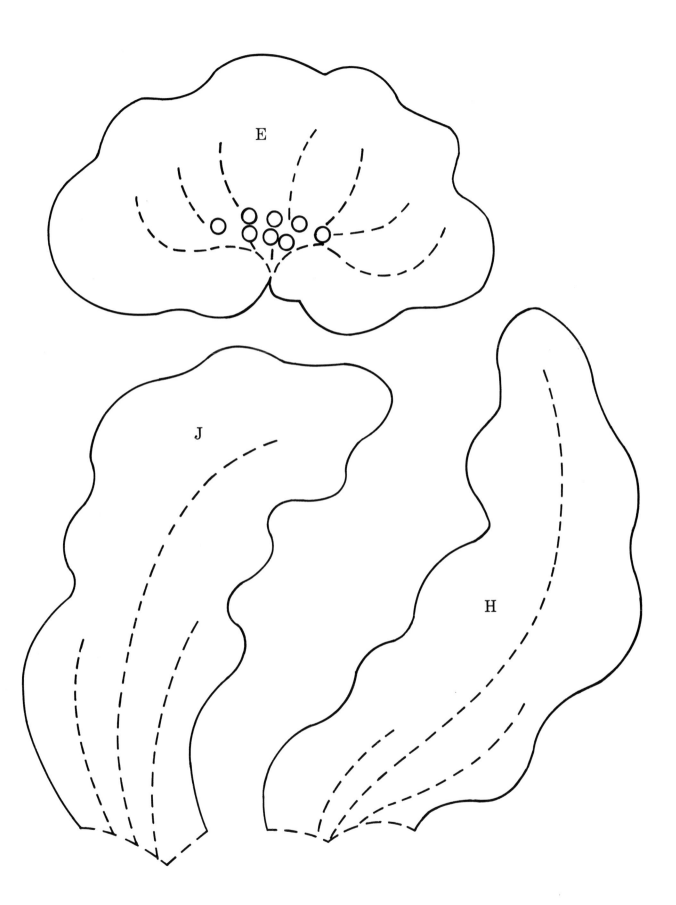

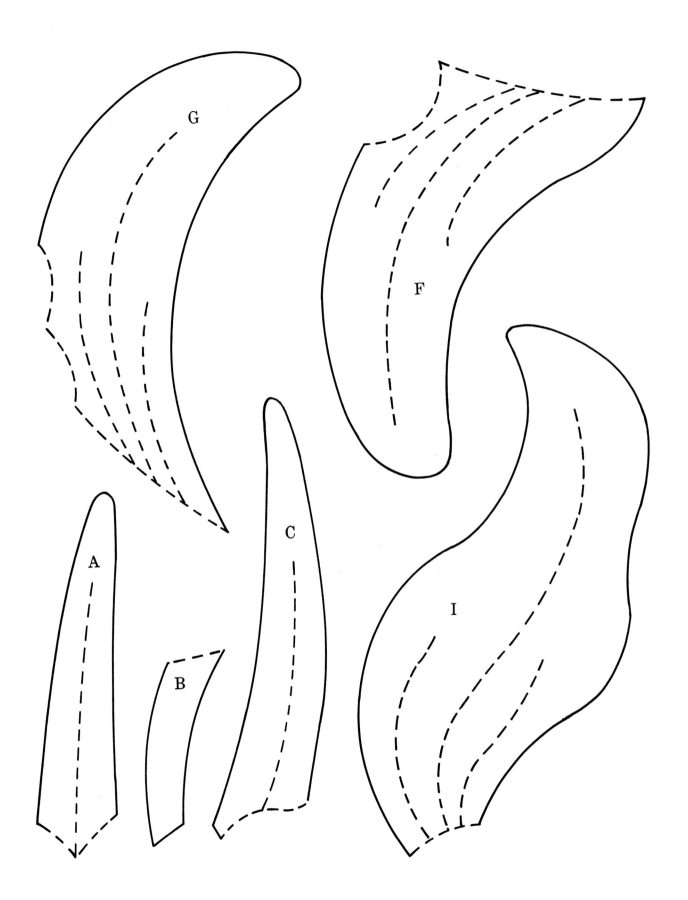

LeMoyne Star

Mrs. Ethel Perry
Cushing, Texas

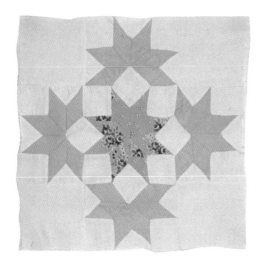

No quilt pattern book would be complete without the most famous diamond-shaped patch of all — the *LeMoyne Star* — and we selected the beauty submitted by Mrs. Perry. She wrote, "After Louisiana was purchased by the United States in 1803, American women called the design the *Lemon Star*, and it began to appear in different parts of the country with varying interpretations."

Mrs. Perry chose to do her star in white and yellow, with the center boasting a bright yellow print.

According to Mrs. Perry, a twin size quilt requires 10 yards of white, 6 yards of solid yellow, 2 yards of yellow print, and, for the border, 1¼ yards of material, preferably of the yellow print. Each block measures approximately 10 inches square.

For one block you will need:
  A — 16 white squares
  B — 32 diamonds (24 solid, 8 print)
  C — 12 white triangles
  D — 4 white squares
Allow ¼ inch for seams on all pattern pieces.

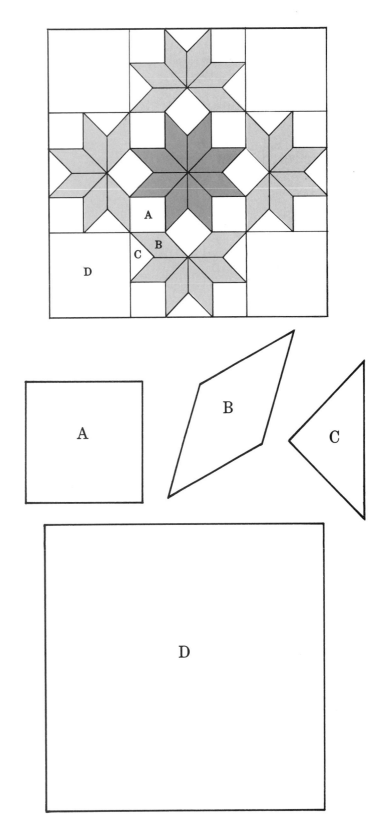

Virginia Star

Ethel M. Martin

Ruston, Louisiana

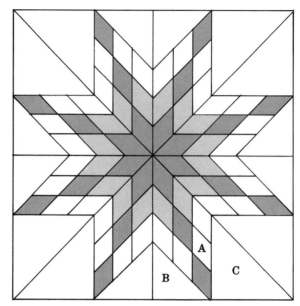

You will find three patterns in this chapter submitted by Mrs. Martin. And for a very good reason: her needlework is so exquisite and her choice of patterns so superb that her creations merit being seen time and time again.

Mrs. Martin wrote, "I have always loved quilts. I pieced my first quilt when I was 8 years old, and started quilting when I was 12 or 13. I quilted for the public from 1953 to 1972 (107 quilts), from *Nine Patches* to fancy *Flower Gardens*. I found quilt making a very relaxing and rewarding hobby."

Being a true authority on the subject, Mrs. Martin said that she uses number 7 between needle and a polyester filling. Beginners will find this pattern easier to execute if they follow the paper technique found in the how-to chapter.

Each block measures about 15½ inches square (plus seam allowances). If you set 30 *Virginia Star* blocks together, 5 across and 6 down, with 2-inch strips between each block and a 2-inch border all around, your finished quilt will measure 89½" x 107".

For one block you will need:
  A — 72 solid diamonds (24 red, 32 blue, 16 yellow)
  B — 8 white triangles
  C — 8 white triangles
Allow ¼ inch for seams on all pattern pieces.

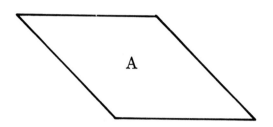

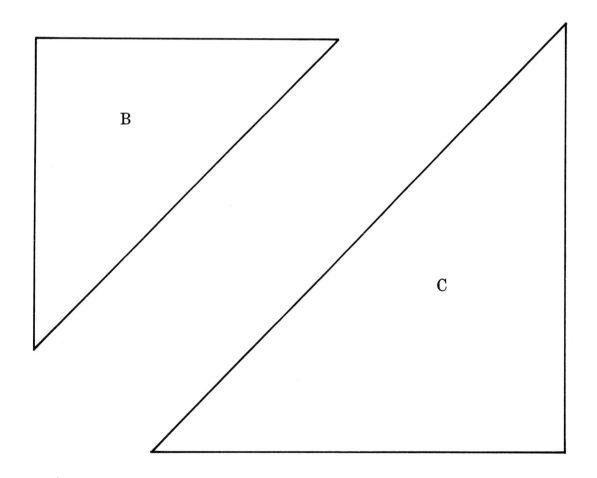

Rosebud

Hester Rofkahr
Clarksville, Arkansas

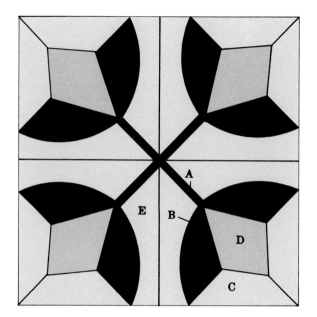

"This beautiful *Rosebud* quilt block pattern has been in my family's possession almost a century, perhaps longer, as I don't know how long my grandmother had it before I first saw it in her home," Mrs. Rofkahr wrote.

Each beautiful block measures 13 inches square (plus seam allowances). Mrs. Rofkahr set her blocks together with 3-inch red strips between each block and 3-inch green squares in the corners. Twenty blocks, set 4 across and 5 down with a 4-inch border all around, will make a quilt 69″ x 85″. It can be used as a coverlet on a double bed or a spread for a twin bed.

For one block you will need:
   A — 4 green stems
   B — 8 green leaves
   C — 8 white pieces
   D — 4 red rosebuds
   E — 8 white pieces
Each pattern piece includes a ¼-inch seam allowance.

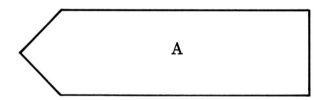

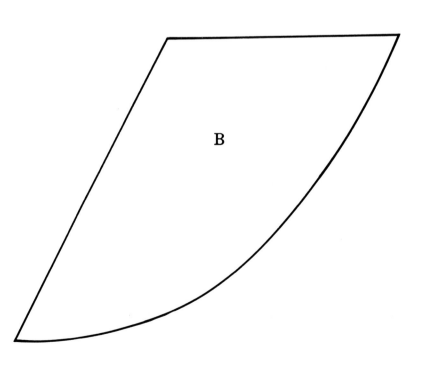

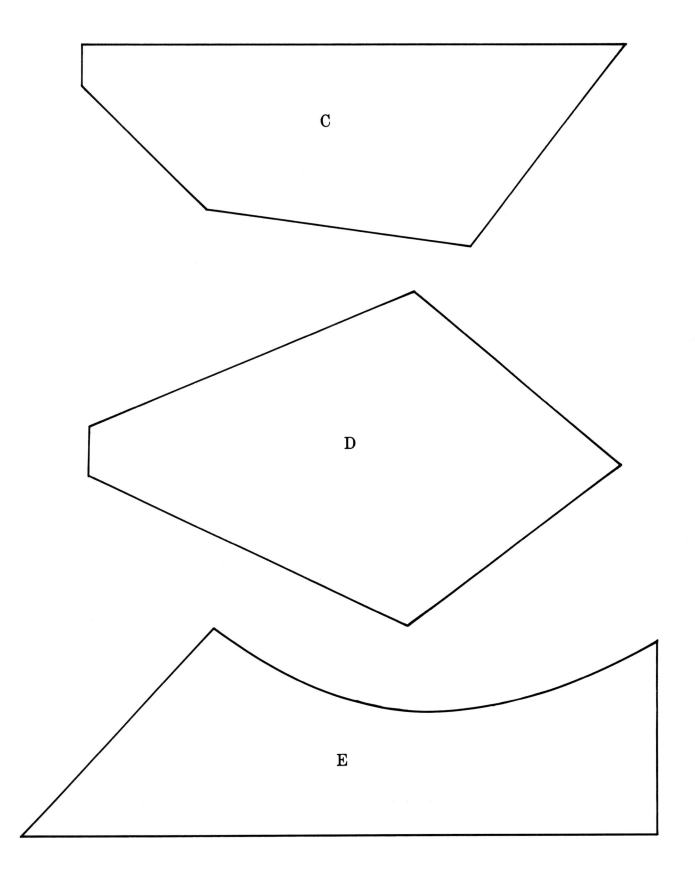

C

D

E

The Drunkard's Path

Lucille Gividen

Sulphur, Kentucky

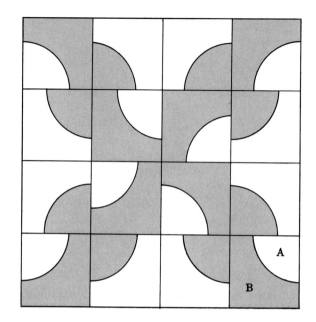

Mrs. Gividen told us that she is a widow with three married children, six grandchildren, and one great-grandchild. When she lost her husband, she found that she had to have a hobby, and she turned to her quilts. What blessed her has blessed her children, and they think the quilts are great, especially when they find so many familiar prints — so many memories of happy days gone by.

Mrs. Gividen said that she spent much of her childhood with a great-grandmother who lived in the mountains of Kentucky. When Mrs. Gividen was a child, she collected a pieced block from each of her great-grandmother's quilts, and all of the patterns Mrs. Gividen has now originated in those Kentucky mountains.

Each pieced block (sixteen 4-inch squares) measures 16 inches square (plus seam allowances). If you place 30 complete blocks 5 across and 6 down with a 5-inch border all around, the finished quilt will measure 90″ x 106″.

For one block you will need:
  A — 16 pieces (8 print, 8 solid)
  B — 16 pieces (8 print, 8 solid)
Allow ¼ inch for seams on all pattern pieces.

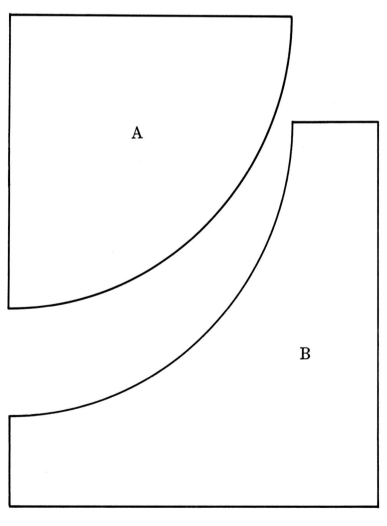

Star and Stirrups

Bessie C. Bowman
Boones Mill, Virginia

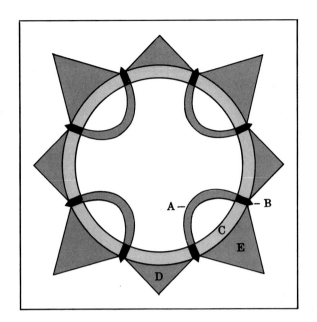

Mrs. Bowman had almost decided not to enter the *Star and Stirrups* pattern in the quilt block contest. "It had such tiny parts," she wrote, "that I did not think anyone would want to make a complete quilt." She did not keep her original measurements.

Well, thank goodness she did share her tiny parts with us, for if you take a block of white material 11 inches square, and mount the pieces as an appliqué, you, too, can have this good-looking quilt pattern.

Bessie's original is made of solid aqua, accompanied by two contrasting prints in aqua and a darker blue. In the center, she has used a four-petaled flower for her quilting pattern.

The patches may be small, but the effect is tremendous!

For one block you will need:
    A — 4 solid pieces
    B — 8 light print pieces
    C — 8 dark print pieces
    D — 4 solid pieces
    E — 4 solid pieces
Allow ¼ inch for seams on all pattern pieces.

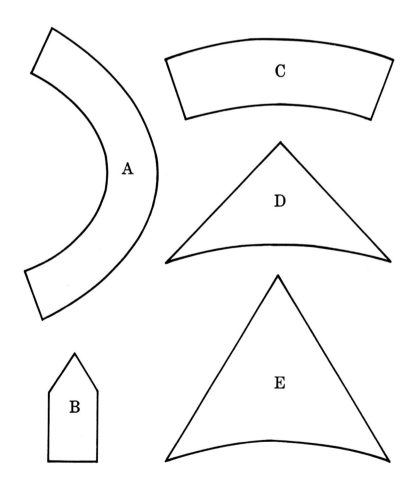

Fancy Dresden Plate

Mrs. Z. E. Cheatham
Evergreen, Virginia

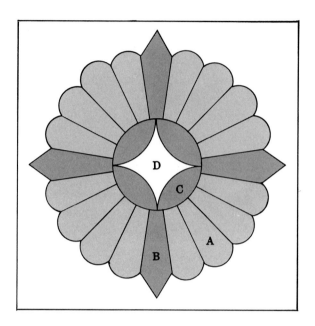

"I have made both silk and cotton *Fancy Dresden Plate* quilts," Mrs. Cheatham wrote. "The silk makes a very lovely bedspread." She used the primary design pieces of the block to bring out the color scheme in her bedroom.

Mrs. Cheatham's block is made of a variety of multicolored prints, appliquéd to a larger square of white polyester crepe. It is a combination pieced and appliquéd quilt, and the quilting pattern alone is enough to mark it as a beauty.

Each of Mrs. Cheatham's blocks measures 17 inches square plus seam allowances. She used 30 blocks, 5 across and 6 down for a lovely quilt. If finished with a 2½-inch border, the quilt will measure approximately 90″ x 107″.

For one block you will need:
   A — 16 print pieces of varying designs
   B — 4 print pieces (this is your major print theme)
   C — 4 print pieces (same print material as B)
   D — this is the shape the center of your block will be after your "plate" is assembled. It is not a pattern piece.
Allow ¼ inch for seams on all pattern pieces.

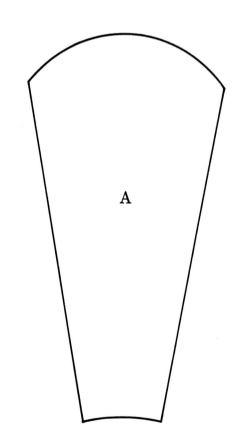

A

110

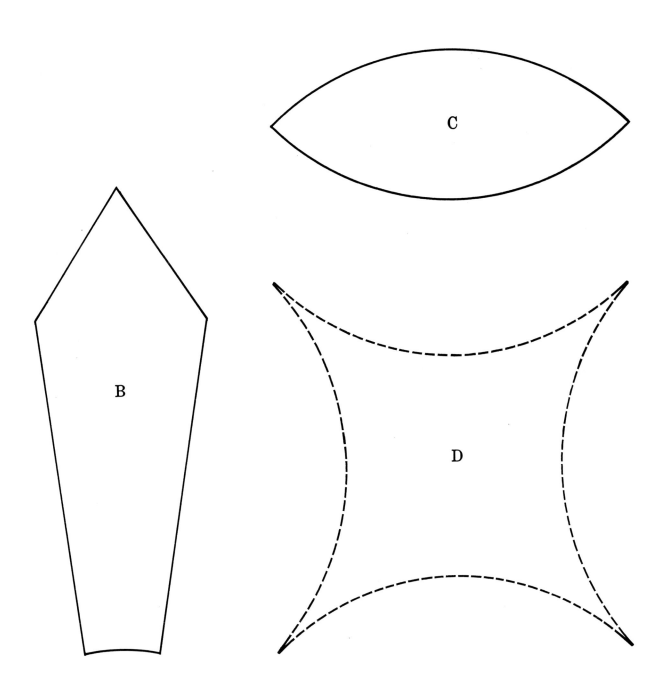

Our Village Green

Mrs. Kermit Crawford
Williford, Arkansas

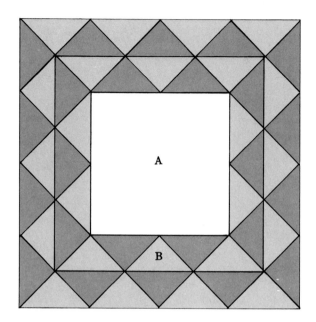

Mrs. Crawford chose for her entry a beautiful old traditional pattern. She used it to make a quilt which she entered in the Mid-South Fair at Memphis last fall — coming out with a prize. "For quilting," she says, "I trace a pretty pattern in the large square, and I quit around the seams of the triangles."

The quilting pattern in the center is a feather circle (or crown), and it is this beautiful needlework that really sets Mrs. Crawford's block apart. She used aqua and a blue and green print for contrast in her block.

Each finished block is 12 inches square (plus seam allowances). Mrs. Crawford used 42 blocks set 6 across and 7 down plus a 3-inch border of triangles or strips to finish the quilt, making it measure approximately 78″ x 90″.

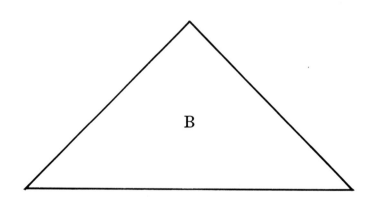

For one block you will need:
   A — 1 white square
   B — 48 triangles (24 solid, 24 print)
Each pattern piece includes a ¼-inch seam allowance.

A

Compass

Mrs. Ollie Miller
Winchester, Kentucky

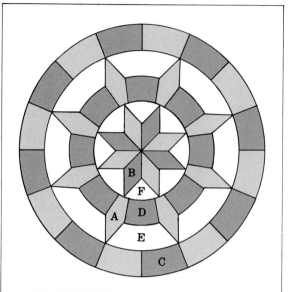

Mrs. Miller said that it might not be of much interest to people, but she just wanted to tell everybody how "the Lord has blessed me with my eyesight, that at 82 years of age, I can still do this kind of work."

Well, if you could see Mrs. Miller's work at close range, you had better believe that she has some pair of eyes. Her work is exquisite, and the overall quilting pattern alone merits the highest praise.

The original block is lovely — soft pink and delicate green with white. Mrs. Miller alternated her pink and green pieces and separated the rings of color with white, making the pattern look like a compass.

Assemble each block beginning with the central star (B), then add the white triangles (F) to make a perfect circle. Next, connect the smallest curved pieces (D) to the white triangles, alternating with diamond-shaped pieces (A). Then connect piece (E) forming another circle, and finally, add a circle of piece (C).

To complete the edges of each block, lay the complete compass circle on a piece of fabric 18 inches square (plus seam allowances) and mark carefully the outside edge.

Cut the square around the curve and into quarters. Four such quarters sewed together will form the frame for your compass. You may find it easier to mount your pattern by appliquéing it directly onto an 18-inch square block of white material.

Twenty such blocks, set 4 across and 5 down with a 3-inch border, will be required to make a quilt 78″ x 96″.

For one block you will need:
    A — 8 pink pieces
    B — 8 diamonds (4 pink, 4 green)
    C — 16 pieces (8 pink, 8 green)
    D — 8 green pieces
    E — 8 white pieces
    F — 8 white pieces
Allow ¼ inch for seams on all pattern pieces.

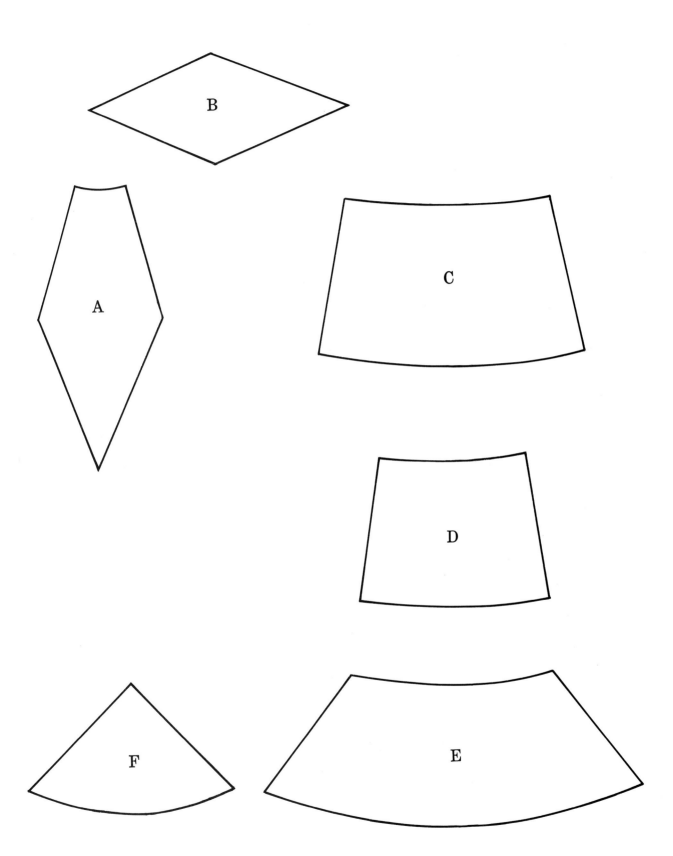

Balloon Girl

Mrs. Joe Bickham
Corpus Christi, Texas

If you have ever seen someone with a fine hand for sewing, it is Mrs. Bickham. She has two patterns in "The Love Patches," and the embroidery alone on both of them is enough to justify their appearance as prize winners. The little girl with the balloons will touch your heart, and Mrs. Bickham said that she thought the pattern was particularly appropriate for a little girl's room.

Each block is 8½″ x 10½″ and may be set together in alternating rows of solid blocks of the same size.

Mrs. Bickham used pale pink for the apron and bonnet and pale blue for the dress with deeper shades of aqua, yellow, and bright pink for the balloons. The detail on the figure is all microscopic embroidery, with little French knots for roses and leaves scattered on the hem and sunbonnet.

Mrs. Bickham suggests changing the effect by using a small check or print for the apron and bonnet.

Allow ¼ inch for seams on all pattern pieces.

117

Tobacco Leaf
Mrs. Z. E. Cheatham
Evergreen, Virginia

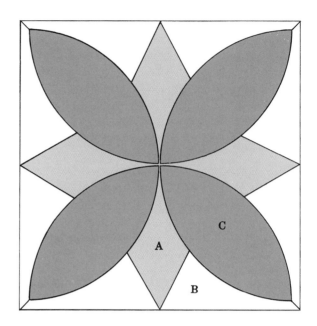

"A neighbor gave me an old square of the *Tobacco Leaf* quilt that her grandmother had made about a hundred years ago," Mrs. Cheatham wrote in sending her entry for the quilt block contest. "I copied it, using the colors as near as I could discern."

Mrs. Cheatham went on to say that she had watched the quilt patterns pictured in *Progressive Farmer* and in several quilt books, but she had never seen this particular one. You must admit, aged or not, it is a grand design for a modern-day quilt.

Mrs. Cheatham is really quite a quilt authority, and she has two patterns in "The Love Patches." She offers this advice to beginners: "Be exact in cutting; don't hurry with quilting, be sure the quilt is square in the frame; machine-stitch the binding to the quilt, but hand-whip down."

Each block measures approximately 14 inches square (plus seam allowances). A quilt 88″ x 105″ requires 30 blocks set 5 across and 6 down with 3-inch strips of dark material between each block and a 3-inch border all around. On each strip, Mrs. Cheatham quilted two 3″ x 6″ tobacco leaf designs, using the color of thread matching the stripping, working a stem through the center.

For one block you will need:
A — 4 pastel pink pieces for the bloom
B — 8 unbleached or very light beige pieces for sandy ground on which bright tobacco grows
C — 4 green leaves (grass green for growing or deep lime for ripe leaves)
Allow 1/4 inch for seams on all pattern pieces.

118

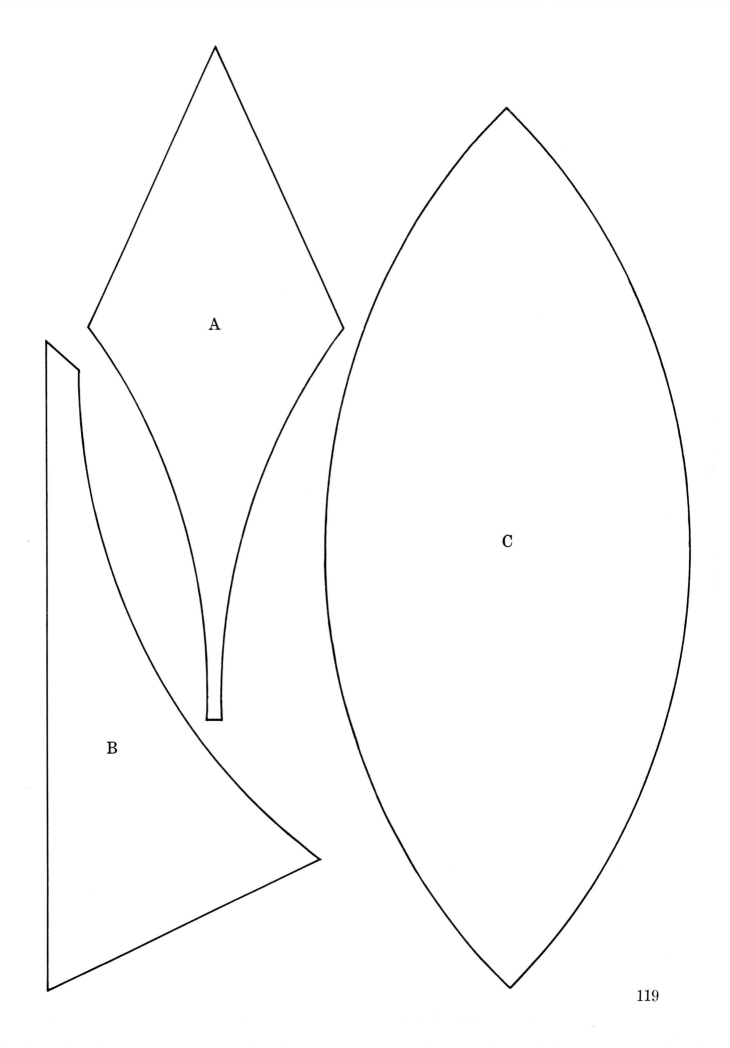

119

Persian Puzzle

Mae L. Wilkinson
Jacksonville, Alabama

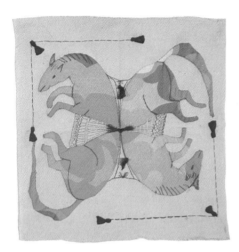

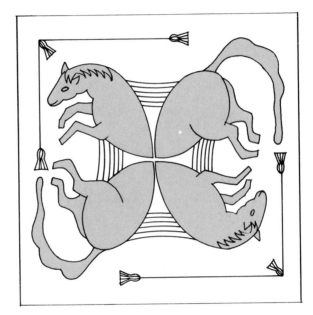

Mrs. Wilkinson entered the *Persian Puzzle* block under the traditional or old-time category, but it was so new and different it made one think it could well be an original.

This pattern would be most suitable for a child's room. It is particularly interesting when half of the twenty-four 15-inch square blocks are appliquéd and half are plain. Actually, this pattern is so fascinating, there are any number of ways one could interpret it — using a wonderful gingham for the horses, for example.

Each block will need 2 heads and 2 tails. They will be arranged in such a way as to show 4 horses. The heads are placed diagonally opposite each other in a counterclockwise position. The tails are diagonally opposite each other, also counterclockwise.

The 2 parts of the horse are connected with rows of herringbone embroidery stitches, which form a saddlecloth for each horse.

The mane, ears, eyes, and mouth are outlined with stitchery. Tassels have been added in the corners and sides of each block.

The horses may be whipped to the muslin square with a blind stitch or buttonhole stitch.

When the quilt blocks are set diagonally with half-blocks finishing the sides, add a border of color 1½ inches all around and then a 4½-inch border of white around the colored border.

Allow ¼ inch for seams on all pattern pieces.

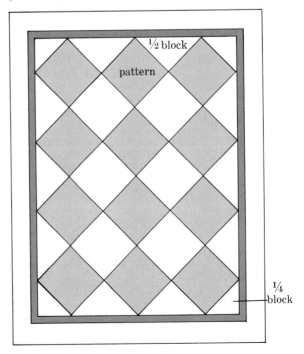

½ block

pattern

¼ block

120

121

Lotts Creek Rose

Mrs. Ollie L. Hurt
Hazard, Kentucky

Mrs. Hurt's exciting appliqué pattern is enough to make a quilt buff out of anybody. And if you could sample her recipe for Cream Pull Candy, you'd want to do all of your quilting over at her house!

Mrs. Hurt uses twelve 20-inch square blocks (plus seam allowances) for her gorgeous quilt. The roses call for 3 yards of red material and 2 yards of green for the leaves. The leaves are first appliquéd on the block, then the rose is appliquéd so that it slightly overlaps the leaves. Individual petals are outlined in embroidery.

After setting the blocks 3 across and 4 down and adding a 6-inch border, Mrs. Hunt's quilt measured approximately 72″ x 92″.

She says that if you would rather use 18-inch blocks of white and use strips between the blocks, that's all right, too. She would rather have one on the 20-inch material, then quilt pretty designs between the blocks.

Apparently Mrs. Hurt's rose quilts are a glorious success, for she has already sold eight.

For one block you will need:
  A — 4 green leaves (pattern reduced to ½ original size)
  B — 1 red rose (pattern reduced to ½ original size)
Allow ¼ inch for seams on all pattern pieces.

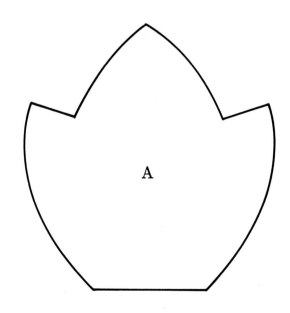

A

122

B

Double Wedding Ring

Maude Stines

Union, South Carolina

Mrs. Stine's *Double Wedding Ring* is the same pattern as *Cathedral Windows,* found elsewhere in "The Love Patches." Yet, by enlarging the design and using only two colors, the effect is quite different — and beautiful.

Mrs. Stines prefers the quilt-as-you-go method, and she selected an unbleached muslin for the larger square and a bright red cotton for the "windows." The result is exquisite, with the crisp white forming petals around each red "window." "It is quite a puzzle," Mrs. Stines wrote, "but once you see a block made, it's really very simple."

Begin with one 8-inch square piece of solid material (this includes seam allowances). If your material is not perfectly square to begin with, your corner folds will not fit together properly. Fold the square diagonally in both directions and mark the center with a pencil point. Press in the ¼-inch seam allowance on all four sides. Fold each corner to the center mark; press flat. Fold the resulting square's corners to the center mark; pin and press flat. Stitch the corner points together in the center with a small +, going through all folded layers. The folded fabric now measures 3¾ inches square.

One quilt block requires 4 folded squares. After completing all 4, attach them by placing right sides together and slip-stitching the edges with matching thread. The assembled quilt block should measure 7½ inches square.

Cut the 2¼-inch square inserts. Set these over the seam lines in the small squares formed by two adjoining larger squares as indicated in the diagram; pin in place. Now fold one edge (it will appear curved when folded) of the "window" square over the inserted patch and slip-stitch it into place with tiny, invisible stitches. Continue doing this on each side of all four square inserts in the center of the quilt block. As you join the assembled blocks together, the side triangular-shaped inserts will become square and will require the same treatment as the 4 center inserts.

Eighty 7½-inch square blocks set 8 across and 10 down will make a quilt 60″ x 75″. The quilt will have half-squares at the edges. You may cut half-patches to insert or leave the edges solid. Mrs. Stines likes to finish her quilt with a deep frill of the red material.

For one block you will need:
 A — 4 square red inserts
 B — 4 large white squares
  (pattern reduced — the block should measure 8 inches square. Dotted lines indicate folds.)
Pattern piece (B) includes a ¼-inch seam allowance.

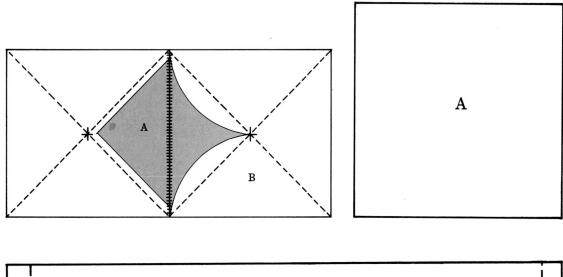

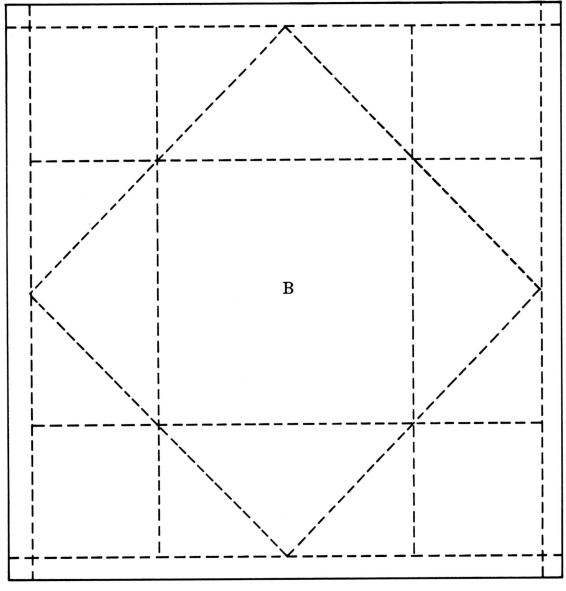

North Carolina Rose

Mrs. Joe Bickham

Corpus Christi, Texas

All through the ages of quilting, the rose has been one of the most readily employed designs, and there are as many varieties of quilt roses as there are roses in a flower catalogue. But no matter how many there are, you won't find a more elegant one than Mrs. Bickham's *North Carolina Rose.*

Each 16½-inch square block (plus seam allowances) has 4 roses of lavender and deep pink. The green leaf is cut from the same pattern as the bud, and she used matching green bias strips for the stems.

Twenty appliquéd blocks and a 7-inch border will make a quilt 80″ x 96½″ if the blocks are set 4 across and 5 down. For her border, the talented Mrs. Bickham just used the same pattern again, running it vinelike around the 4 sides.

For one block you will need:
- A — 4 green stems
- B — 4 deep pink buds
- C — 20 green leaves (includes area piece B)
- D — 4 lavender outer petals
- E — 4 deep pink inner petals
- F — 4 yellow centers

Allow ¼ inch for seams on all pattern pieces.

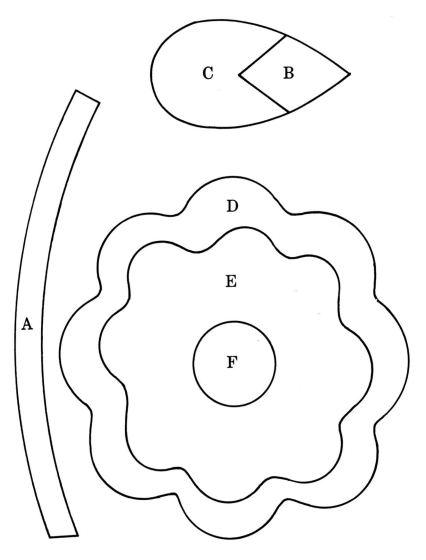

126

Flower Garden

Mrs. George Steed
Lineville, Alabama

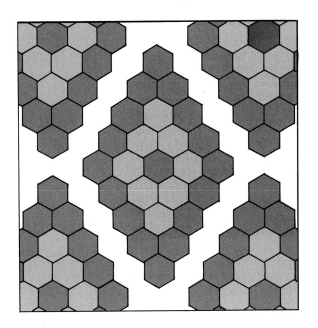

"The Love Patches" is a veritable garden of Ruth Steed's quilts, and *Flower Garden* is just one of her bouquets.

The *Flower Garden* quilts had their origin back in the twelfth century when fine English needlework with mosaic patterns pieced in minute patches flourished. The English have always loved flowers and gardens, and it was from them that the seeds of our *Flower Garden* quilt were sown.

Mrs. Steed's hexagonal pattern is particularly beautiful, and it is one of those delightful ones to quilt-as-you-go. Using wonderful floral prints of gorgeous hues, the pattern requires 82 full flower designs, each one 12 inches long and 7½ inches wide, with 25 hexagons (16 print, 9 solid). The quilt is filled with half-hexagons at the top and bottom, and the sides are left scalloped from the floral pieces.

Mrs. Steed says this pattern makes up particularly well for a coverlet, and a contrasting dust ruffle will provide a border for your flowers.

The pattern piece includes a ¼-inch seam allowance.

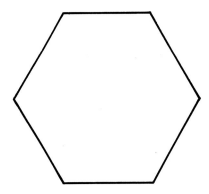

Monkey Wrench

Mrs. Jewell Boitnott
Rocky Mount, Virginia

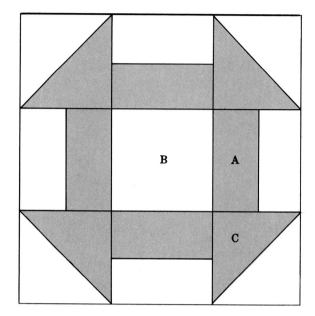

For a traditional, old-time pattern, and one that is particularly good for someone just beginning to quilt, Mrs. Boitnott chose a wonderful print of yellow, orange, lavender, and blue to go with her dark green solid. The effect is gorgeous and would be stunning with any decor.

Mrs. Boitnott said that it was really her mother's pattern and that she had had it for several years.

The blocks measure approximately 12¾ inches square and could easily be set together with strips of the solid color. A matching border of bright green wouldn't go amiss, either.

For one block you will need:
   A — 8 rectangles (4 solid,
       4 print)
   B — 1 print square
   C — 8 triangles (4 solid,
       4 print)
Each pattern piece includes a ¼-inch seam allowance.

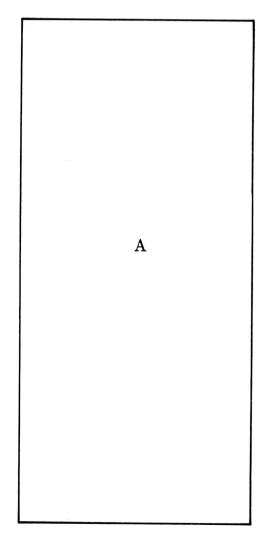

A

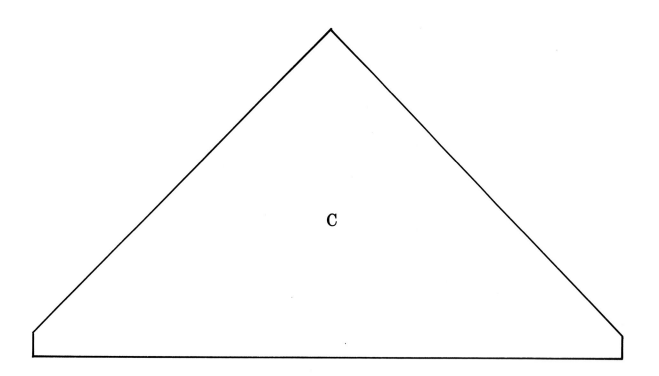

C

B

129

Buck 'n' Wing

Mrs. Myrtle Aldridge

Glen Allen, Alabama

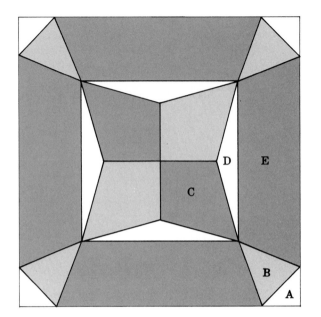

In pioneer days, the square dance was a popular form of recreation. On these occasions, couples would keep lively time to the music in a dance called the "Buck 'n' Wing" or "Buck Dance." Mrs. Aldridge wrote "My husband and I often attend old-time string music sessions and he likes to cut the 'Buck 'n' Wing.' This was my inspiration for originating this quilt block."

Each block measures approximately 9½ inches square (plus seam allowances). To make a quilt 85″ x 98½″, set 42 blocks 6 across and 7 down with a 4-inch border all around.

For one block you will need:
   A — 4 light triangles
   B — 4 yellow print triangles
   C — 4 diamonds (2 red,
          2 yellow print)
   D — 4 light pieces
   E — 4 red print pieces
Allow ¼ inch for seams on all pattern pieces.

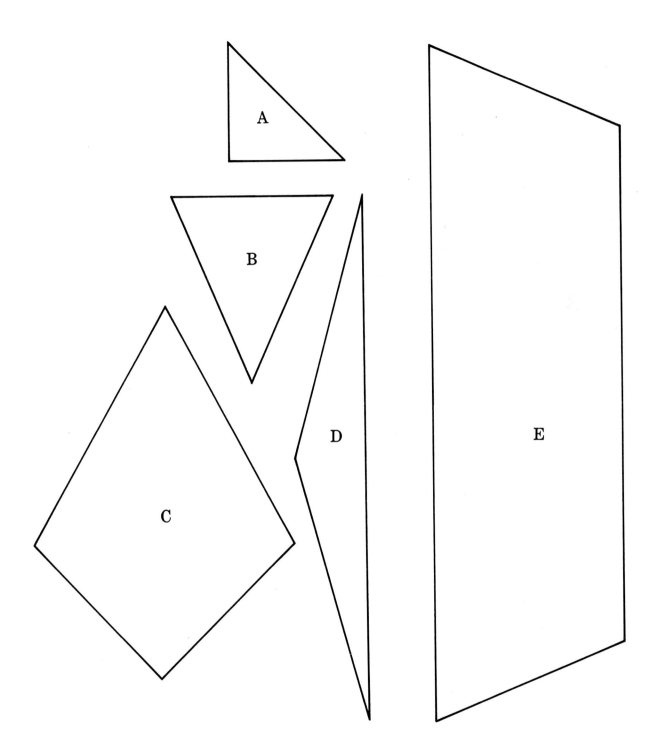

Sunflower

Mrs. Emory M. DeBusk
Urbanna, Virginia

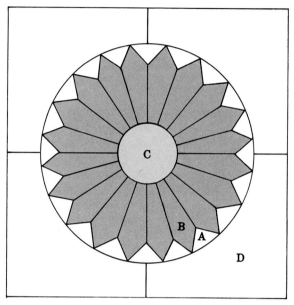

As a young girl in the mountains of West Virginia (Monroe County), I used to watch my mother and her neighbors during winter days piece their quilts, then eagerly put them in frames for quilting," Jessie DeBusk wrote. "How they enjoyed seeing the quilt completed square by square. Some were quite pretty, others were made for service as comforts (with wool filling, some carded by me). For some reason I never fell heir to any of the pretty quilts, but I do have some of the wool comforts. Guess this is where I inherited my desire for quilting."

"Someday," she said, "I hope to have a handmade quilt on each of my beds and I want to enjoy making them myself."

The pattern she chose for her contest entry has always been one of her favorites, and she particularly liked it because the *Sunflower*'s colors could be coordinated to blend with almost any decor. The pattern is also known as *Dresden Plate, Bride's Quilt,* and *The Friendship.*

Each block is 15 inches square (plus seam allowances). A double size quilt measuring 87″ x 105″ will take 30 blocks set 5 across and 6 down with 3-inch strips between each block.

For one block you will need:
A — 20 triangles
B — 20 petals
C — 1 center circle
D — 4 pieces
Allow 1/4 inch for seams on all pattern pieces.

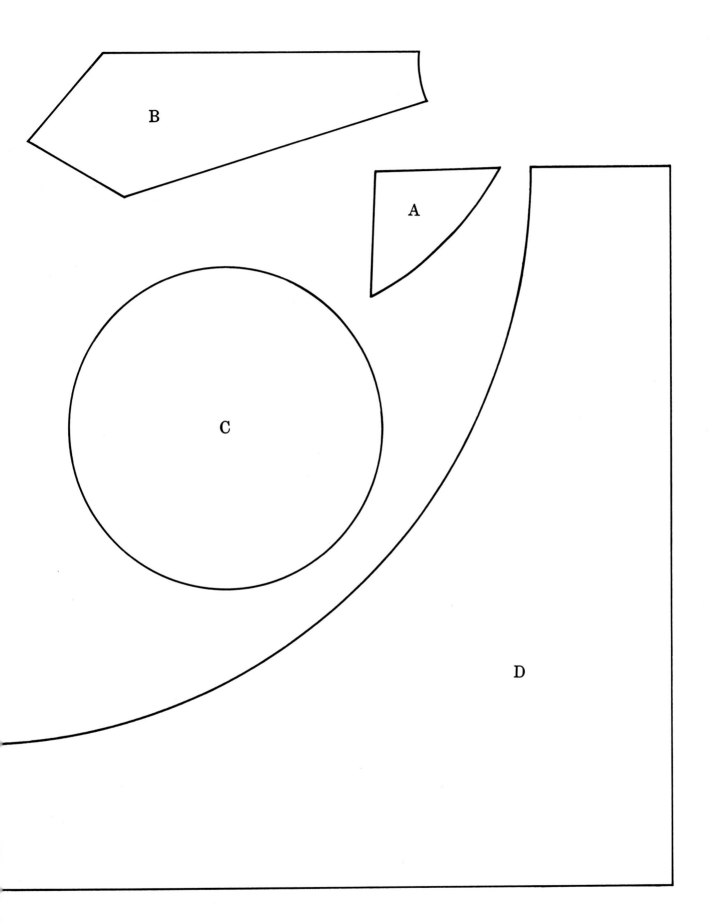

B

A

C

D

The Great-Grandmother Quilt

Mrs. Ruby Rutan

Red House, West Virginia

Mrs. Rutan regrets that she does not know the actual amount of material needed to make her beautiful pattern. However, she did say that she thought it would be safe to use 2 yards each of the red and green and 7 yards of the white.

Using a white background, Mrs. Rutan appliquéd twelve 18-inch square blocks (plus seam allowances). She set 3 across and 4 down with 8-inch strips between each block and suggests finishing the quilt with a 5-inch border. The quilt measures 80″ x 106″.

For one block you will need:
- A — 4 red pieces
- B — 4 small green leaves
- C — 4 large green leaves
- D — 1 red piece

Allow ¼ inch for seams on all pattern pieces.

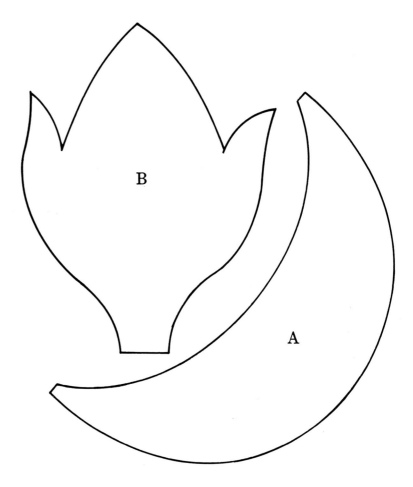

134

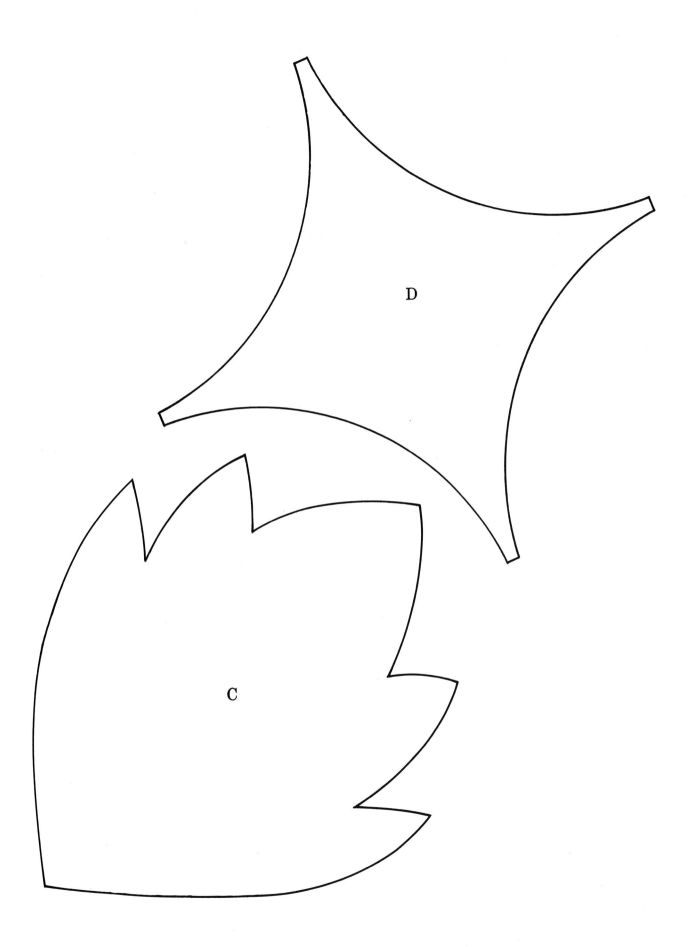

D

C

Milky Way

Ethel M. Martin
Ruston, Louisiana

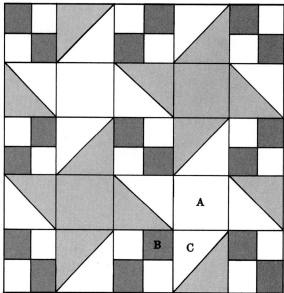

This simple pattern, a classic, was chosen by Mrs. Martin because the completed effect is one of such beauty. She used white, gold, and blue for her colors, but it would be equally lovely in any number of combinations. This particular pattern would be highly desirable for a boy's room, for it is so geometrically fascinating.

Each block measures approximately 12½ inches square. *Milky Way* lends itself beautifully to a central-medallion type of quilt. Take 6 of the pieced blocks, center them (2 across and 3 down), and add a strip of blue 12 inches wide all around the center design. Since the pieced blocks are the focal point, the way you work the remainder of your borders will be up to you. The medallion may be made by moving the 6 star blocks to any design.

For one block you will need:
  A — 4 squares (2 white, 2 gold)
  B — 36 squares (18 white, 18 blue)
  C — 24 triangles (12 white, 12 gold)
Each pattern piece includes a ¼-inch seam allowance.

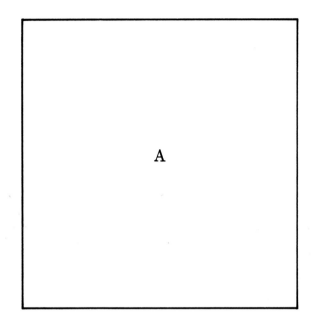

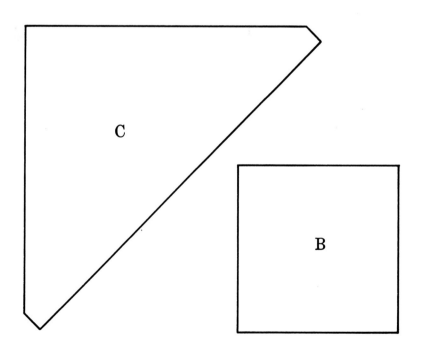

New York Beauty

Ruth K. Palmer

Niota, Tennessee

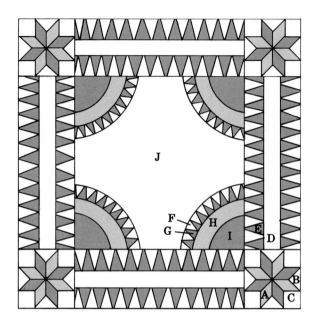

Mrs. Palmer's beautiful quilt block brings to mind the winter ice and midnight sun of distant places. Her pattern is large enough (approximately 31½ inches square) that a single block could be used for a bridge table cover or a large pillow.

For one block you will need:
- A — 32 diamonds (16 yellow, 16 orange)
- B — 16 white triangles
- C — 16 white squares
- D — 4 white strips (18 inches long)
- E — 192 triangles (96 orange — 8 cut in half lengthwise, 96 white).
- F — 36 white triangles
- G — 36 orange triangles (4 cut in half lengthwise)
- H — 4 yellow pieces
- I — 4 orange pieces
- J — 1 white piece (pattern reduced — dotted lines indicate folds and each should measure 10⅛ inches long)

Allow ¼ inch for seams on all pattern pieces.

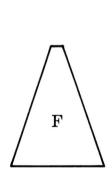

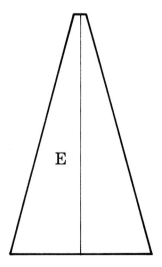

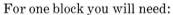

138

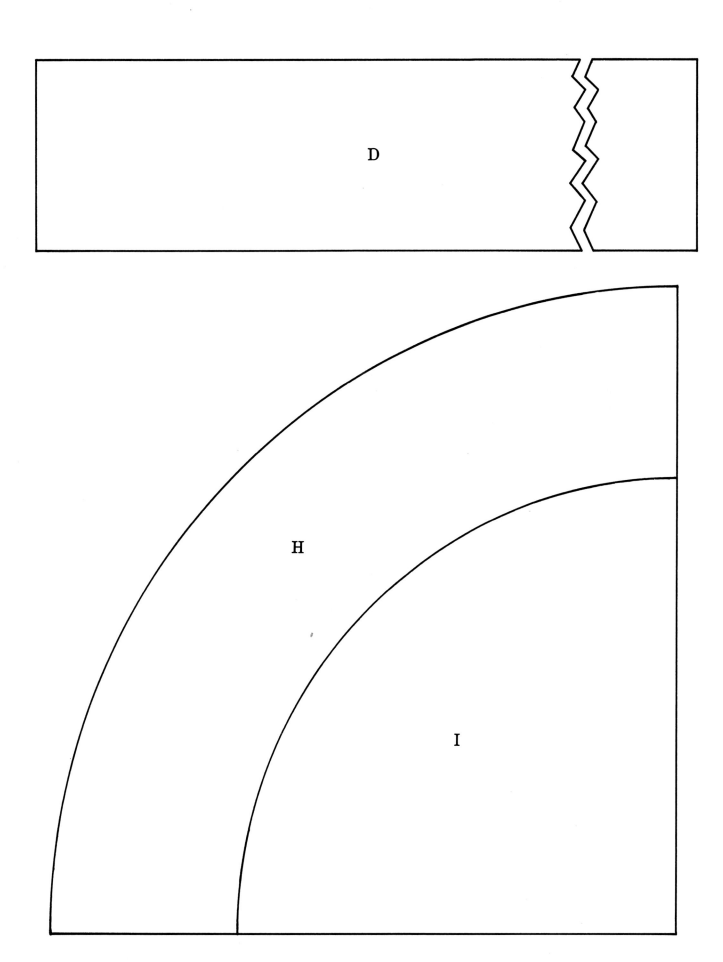

D

H

I

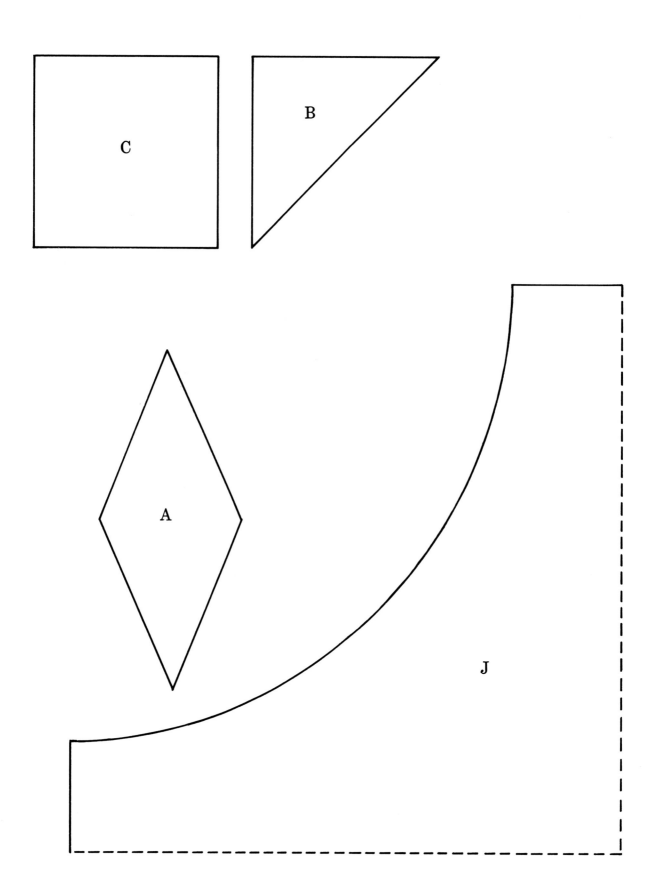

Eight-Point Star

Lala C. Erwin
Cumberland, Virginia

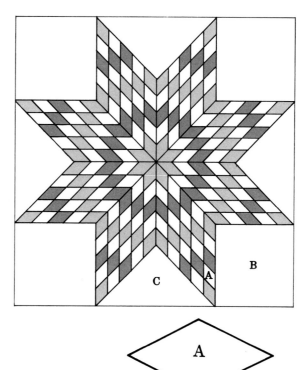

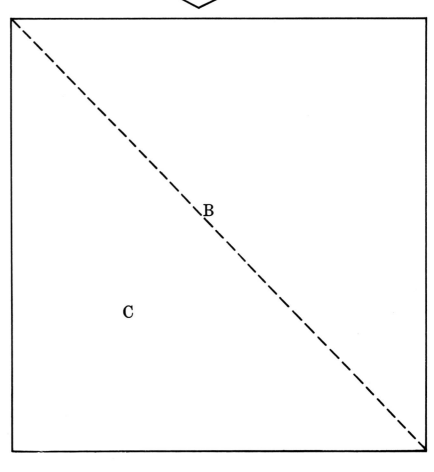

Mrs. Erwin pieced her beautiful star from a pattern she cut from a quilt her grandmother made. Mrs. Erwin wrote, "I am sure the quilt is a hundred or more years old, for it has a homespun lining."

The pattern could very well be that old, for stars have always been a favorite pattern with quilters. But Mrs. Erwin's interpretation in red, white, and blue, is just as modern as tomorrow with its geometric perfection.

The paper technique described in the how-to chapter would be particularly helpful for an intricate design such as this. The diamonds must all be the exact size in order to fit together.

Each block measures approximately 15½ inches square (plus seam allowances). For a quilt 70½" x 92" you will need 12 star blocks set 3 across and 4 down with 6-inch strips between each block and a 6-inch border all the way around.

For one block you will need:
- A — 200 diamonds (56 red, 96 white, 48 blue)
- B — 4 squares (includes area of triangle C)
- C — 4 triangles

Allow ¼ inch for seams on all pattern pieces.

141

Turkey Track

Marguerite Woods
Brooks, Georgia

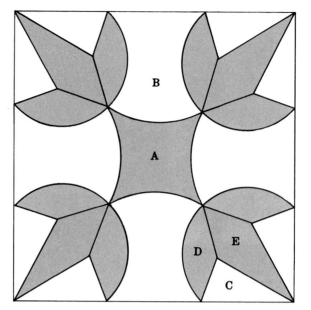

One of the truly traditional patterns is this beautiful one from Miss Woods. It was popular over two hundred years ago, and will probably be in demand two hundred years from now.

Miss Woods wrote that "the traditional arrangement of this design is an alternation of plain and pieced blocks." Beginners might find the pattern easier to assemble if they follow the paper technique described in the how-to chapter.

Make 80 blocks, each approximately 9 inches square (plus seam allowances); sew 8 across and 10 down. A 9-inch border all around will make the finished quilt 90" x 108".

For one block you will need:
    A — 1 print piece
    B — 4 white pieces
    C — 8 white triangles
    D — 8 print pieces
    E — 4 print diamonds
Allow ¼ inch for seams on all pattern pieces.

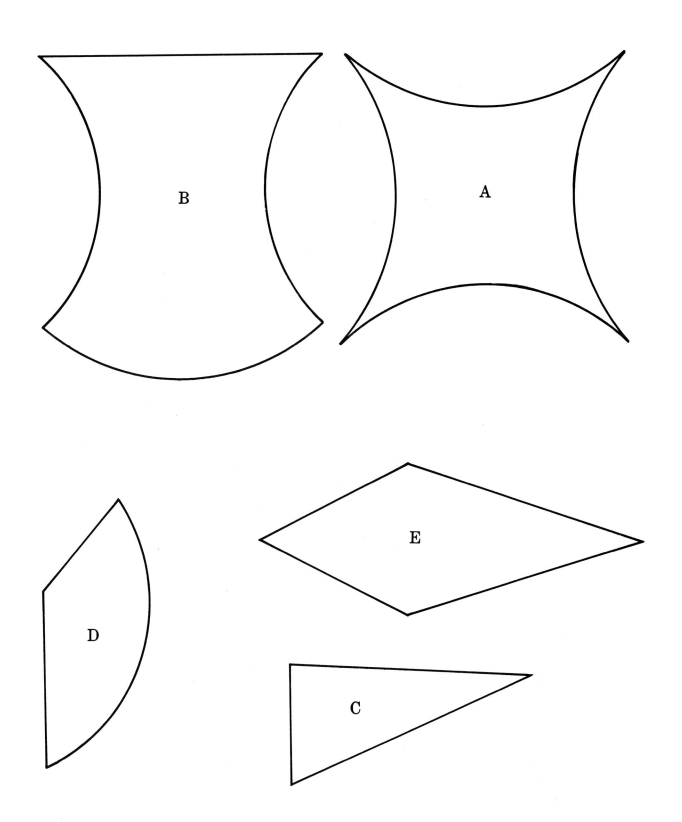

Jack-in-the-Box

Gladys Clavin
Billings, Oklahoma

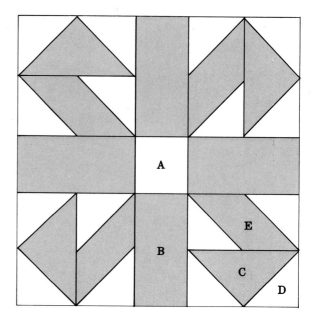

We had a selection of patterns when it came to Mrs. Gladys Clavin, for she sent in three to the quilt block contest, and any one of them would have been essential to a quilt pattern book.

"I'm sorry I can't claim credit for designing any of these patterns," she wrote. "They are from our family collection and I have no idea as to their designer. My mother, Mrs. Iva Bailery, loved and made quilts until she was 92. These were in her collection which I now have."

Using 12 1/2-inch square blocks (plus seam allowances), you will need 56 blocks (29 pieced, 28 plain) alternately set 7 across and 8 down with a 3-inch border, to make a quilt 93 1/2" x 106".

For one block you will need:
    A — 1 white square
    B — 4 red rectangles
    C — 4 red triangles
    D — 16 white triangles
    E — 4 red pieces
Each pattern piece includes a 1/4-inch seam allowance.

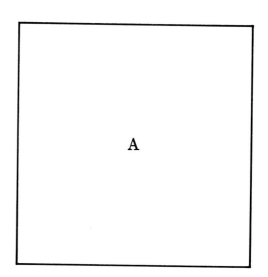

A

144

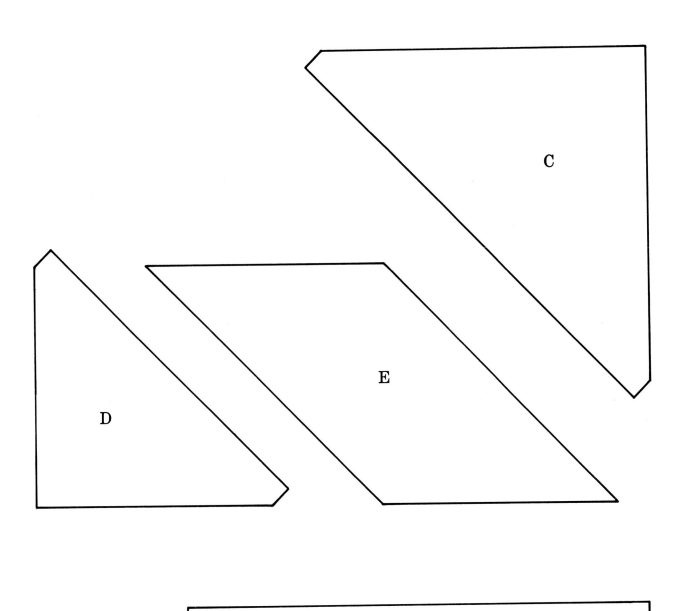

Wild Rose

Mrs. Rex Watson
Valparaiso, Indiana

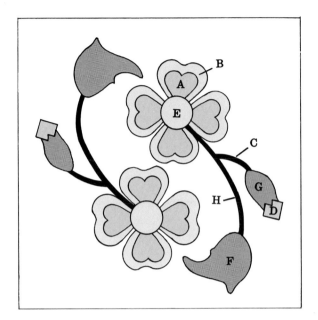

"I chose the *Wild Rose* pattern because it makes such a beautiful quilt, and it brings back memories of girlhood days on the farm, where we had the delicate wild rose blooming along the fence row."

Mrs. Watson's wild roses are so lifelike we just wish you could see them for yourself.

Mrs. Watson loves to piece quilts and has made a number of them during the past three years. Working in a yard goods department of a store keeps her pretty busy, but she particularly enjoys buying fabrics for the store.

These are Mrs. Watson's directions:

Place the appliqué design on an 18-inch square block of white (plus seam allowances) in the position shown in the sketch, after each piece is turned under about 1/4 inch. Narrow bias fold will make the stem.

A quilt about 78″ x 96″ using a 3-inch border will require 20 blocks set 4 across and 5 down. You will need 5 yards of white, 2 yards of pink for outer petals, 1 yard of rose, 1/6 yard of yellow for centers, and 2/3 yard of green. Quilt

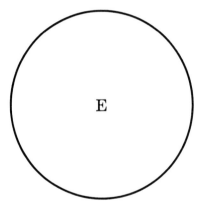

around center, each petal, stems, leaves, and a vein or two in each of the leaves.

For one block you will need:
  A — 8 rose petals
  B — 8 pink petals
  C — 2 green stems
  D — 2 rose squares
  E — 2 yellow circles
  F — 2 green leaves
  G — 2 green buds
  H — 2 green stems
Allow 1/4 inch for seams on all pattern pieces.

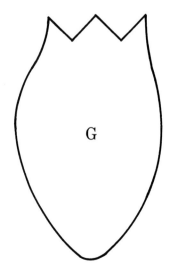

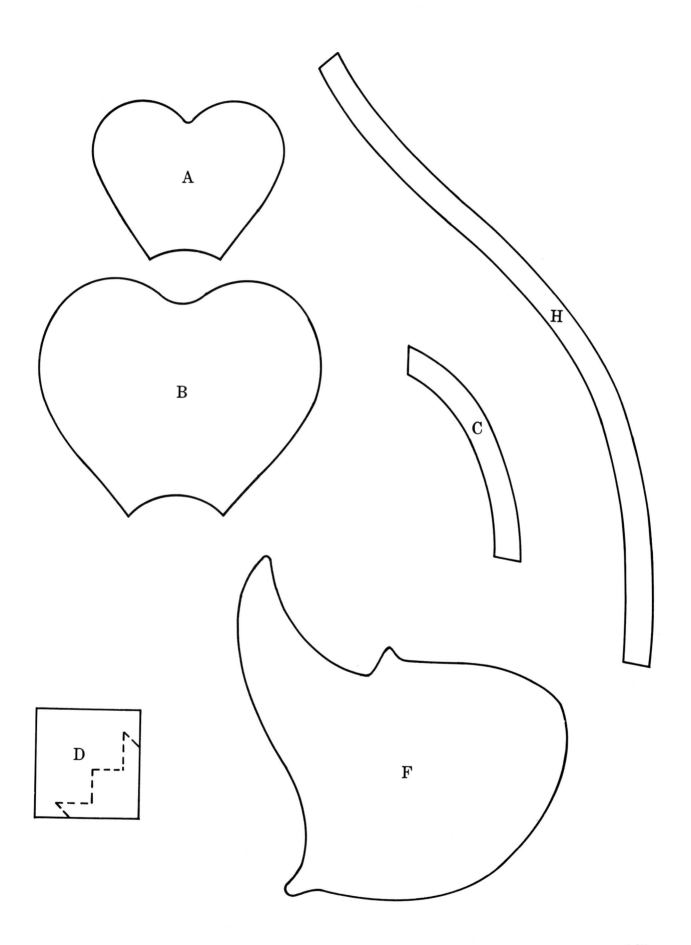

147

Aunt Eliza's Star

Mrs. Nova Lowe
Hayesville, North Carolina

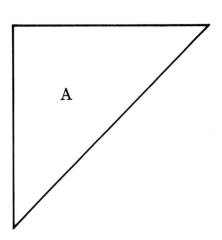
Mrs. Lowe will be well represented in the quilting world when *Award Winning Quilts* meets the public, for she has two patterns in this book. For this one, she chose an old-time, traditional pattern, and her block is nothing short of stunning.

Instead of keeping her star in the perfunctory red, white, and blue combination, she included a butter pecan color to take the place of the blue. This, combined with a brilliant lipstick red and a crisp white, just had to be considered a shining example of a shooting star. The quilting alone would make it a knockout, and we just wish you could see her block, rather than having to vicariously enjoy it.

Each block measures about 15 inches square. For this pattern, Mrs. Lowe said that she used 3 yards of white, 3⅓ yards of beige, and 1½ yards of red. A full-size quilt will require 30 of the blocks set 5 across and 6 down, and she bound her quilt in red.

For one block you will need:
   A — 12 solid triangles (4 white, 8 red)
   B — 8 solid squares (4 white, 4 red)
   C — 1 white square
   D — 4 beige rectangles
Allow ¼ inch for seams on all pattern pieces.

B

C

D

149

Grandmother's Engagement Ring

Madge Byrd
Poyen, Arkansas

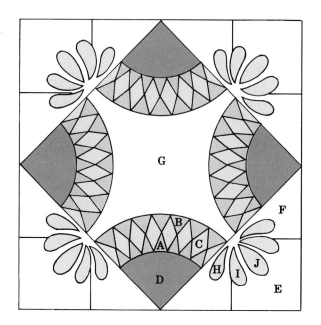

According to Miss Byrd, this pattern was once called *The Tear Drop*. Whatever the name, her arrangement is beautiful and her color selection and interpretation make it an original.

This particular design employs both piecing and appliqué. Pieces (H), (I), and (J) are appliquéd in place after the block has been assembled.

Each block measures 18 inches square (plus seam allowances). For a quilt 90″ x 108″ you will need 30 such blocks set 5 across and 6 down.

Miss Byrd advises beginners to beware: the pattern is not an easy one. The number of pieces involved makes the design difficult to execute.

For one block you will need:
  A — 28 brown triangles
  B — 28 brown triangles
  C — 28 print diamonds (4 cut in
      half lengthwise)
  D — 4 dark brown pieces
  E — 4 beige squares
  F — 8 beige triangles
  G — 1 beige piece (dotted line
      indicates fold)
  H — 8 print petals
  I — 8 print petals
  J — 4 print petals
Allow ¼ inch for seams on all pattern pieces.

150

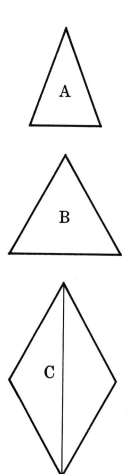

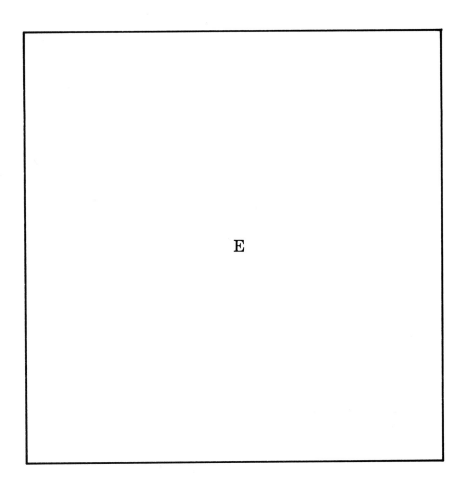

E

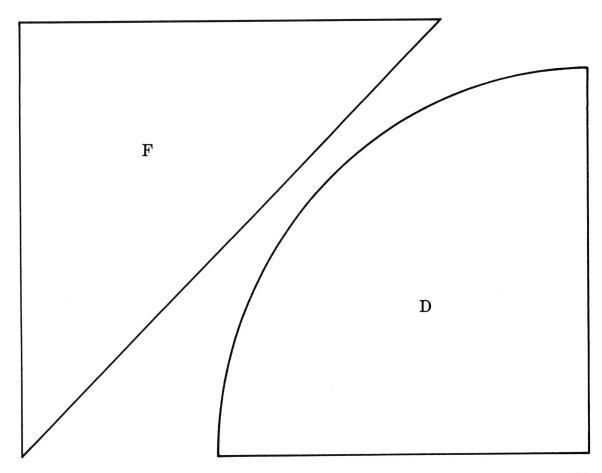

F

D

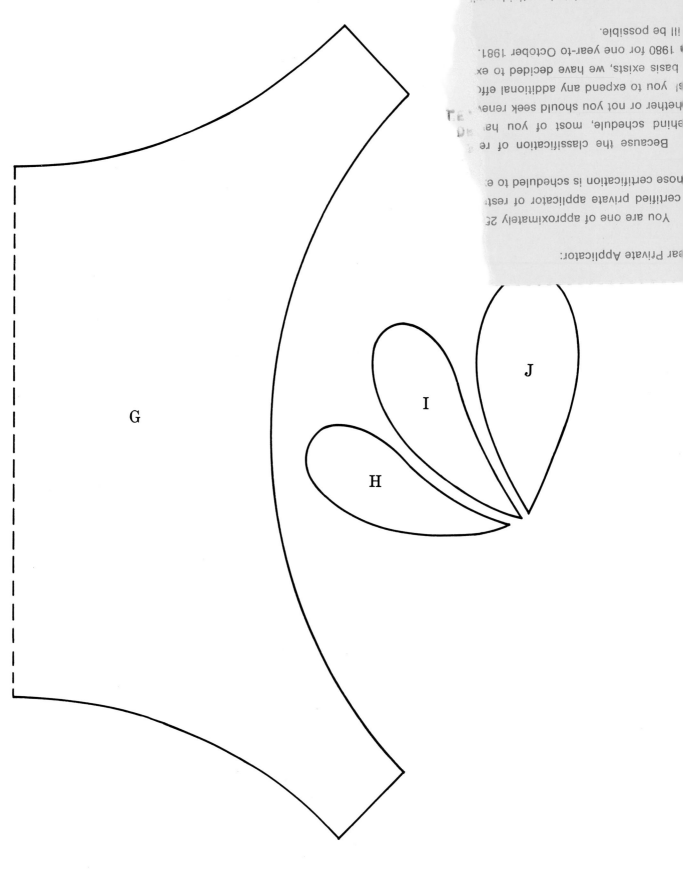

Pieced Star

Mrs. Henry Teague
Eddyville, Kentucky

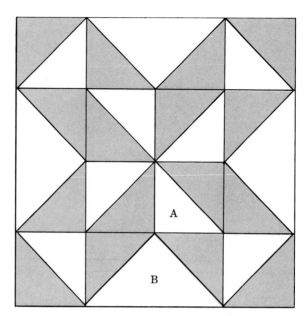

We had three wonderful patterns from Mrs. Teague to choose from, and we selected the star because of its popularity throughout quilting time.

The quilt block made by Mrs. Teague is an old classic, and she chose for her print one that could well recall colonial days. Strangely enough, these are the prints that are the most in demand for today's quilting patterns, and they are the most difficult to come by. Any number of quilting women will say to you, "If you ever run across such and such a print, let me know where you find it." And that goes for the one submitted by Mrs. Teague. The print of red and white and shades of blue and yellow is truly a quilter's dream.

The block for *Pieced Star* measures approximately 11 inches square (plus seam allowances), and a quilt 77" x 88" will require 28 pieced blocks and 28 plain ones, alternately set 7 across and 8 down. You will need about 3½ yards of colonial print, and 5½ yards of white fabric.

For one block you will need:
  A — 24 triangles (8 white, 16 print)
  B — 4 white triangles
Allow ¼ inch for seams on all pattern pieces.

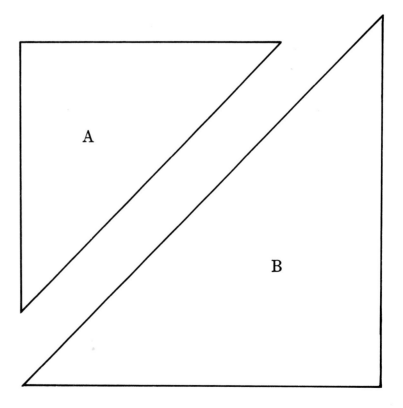

153

Hands All Around

Mrs. Ollie Miller
Winchester, Kentucky

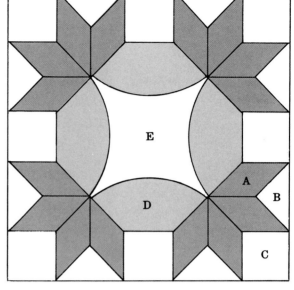

There are two things Mrs. Miller particularly likes to do: she likes to use pink and green combinations in her quilts and she likes to square dance. Well, if you like to quilt, you can't go wrong following the directions for Mrs. Miller's beautiful pattern.

Each of her blocks measures 14½ inches square (plus seam allowances). You may wish to alternate pieced blocks with plain ones. By setting 20 blocks 4 across and 5 down and adding a 6-inch double border using pink and green, your quilt should measure 70″ x 84½″.

For one block you will need:
  A — 16 green diamonds
  B — 8 white triangles
  C — 8 white squares
  D — 4 pink pieces
  E — 1 white piece
Allow ¼ inch for seams on all pattern pieces.

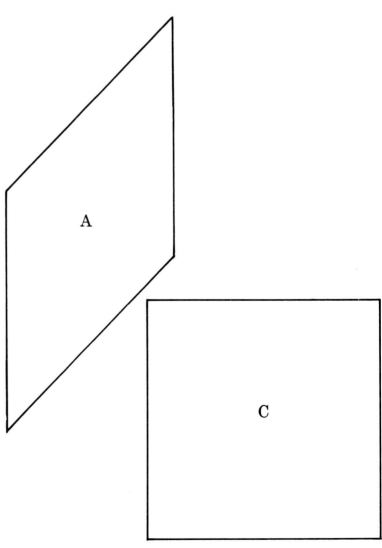

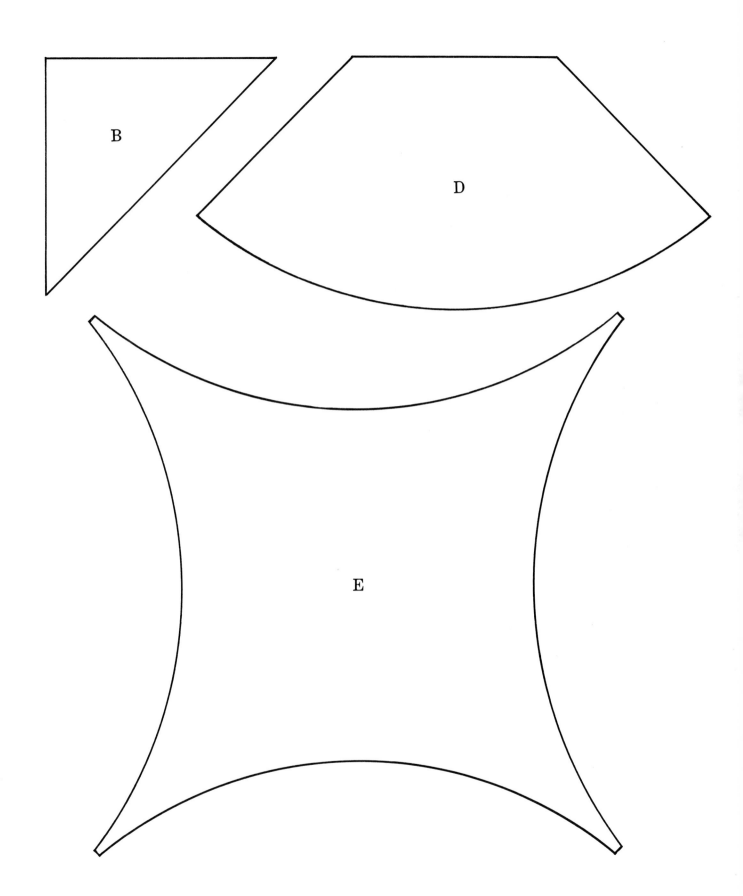

B

D

E

155

Four T's

Mrs. Louis Dilmore
Cottondale, Florida

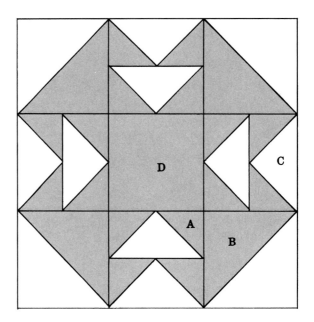

Mrs. Dilmore is 70 years old and she chose for her quilt block entry a famous old quilt pattern sometimes called *The Double T*. "My great-grandmother Cremer gave me this pattern when I was 12 years old," she wrote. "I enjoy piecing up my scraps and making pretty quilts."

Mrs. Dilmore has 4 children, 13 grandchildren, and 8 great-grandchildren. She made 5 quilts for each of her children, 2 each for the grandchildren, and she has now started on quilts for her great-grandchildren.

"In all my quilt making," she said, "I have never made more than 2 quilts alike. I just love quilt making and I am happy to share my pattern with others."

For a double bed, Mrs. Dilmore says it will take thirty 15-inch square quilt blocks. After putting them all together, she finishes the quilt with a 1½-inch border.

Mrs. Dilmore buys 5 yards of material for the backing. She used 2½ pounds of cotton batt for the filling, and she quilts all of her creations by the quilt-as-you-go method.

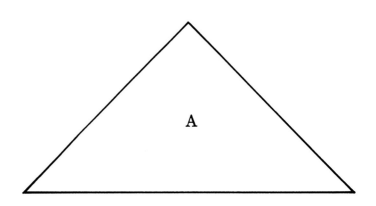

For one block you will need:
A — 16 red triangles
B — 8 triangles (4 light, 4 red)
C — 8 light triangles
D — 1 red square
Allow ¼ inch for seams on all pattern pieces.

156

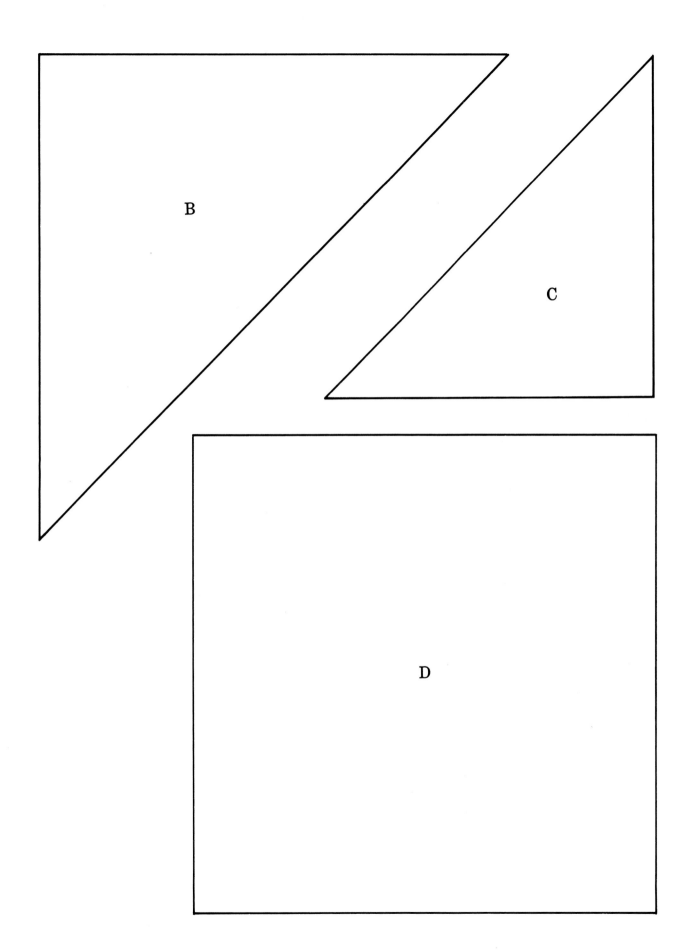

B

C

D

Double Wedding Ring

Mrs. Coy Williams
Telford, Tennessee

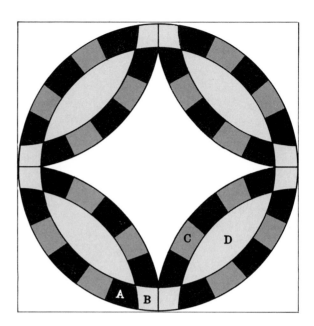

Mrs. William's pattern is a variation on an old-time, traditional pattern using appliqué and piecing.

The overall size of the muslin quilt block is approximately 19½ inches square. Mrs. Williams chose red for the plain patches, and 4 different prints in green, yellow, blue, and pink for the wedge-shape pieces. The most important thing to remember is that she used the same print next to her predominant solid color — in this instance, a green print next to the solid red.

Incidentally, Mrs. Williams has a word to the wise: she would advise you not to try the pattern unless you are familiar with the ceremony — of quilting, that is.

For one block you will need:
- A — 16 green print pieces to go next to the red (8 pieces cut with the pattern reversed)
- B — 8 plain red pieces
- C — 24 print pieces (3 different prints between the green prints)
- D — 4 solid pieces (this may be omitted as part of the background, or used as a color different from the background)

Each pattern piece includes a ¼-inch seam allowance.

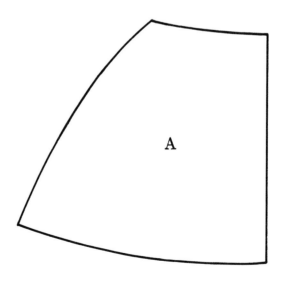

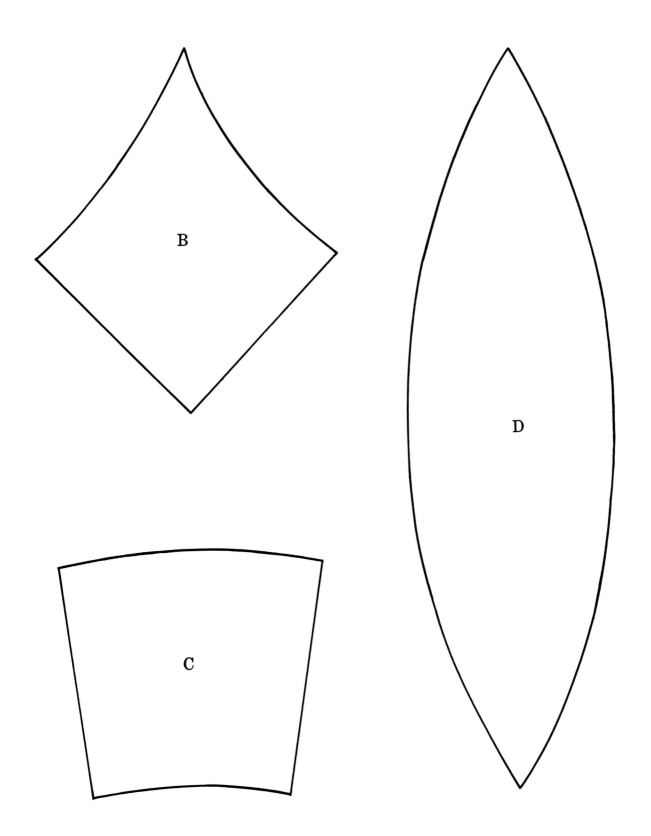

Blazing Star

Ethel M. Martin

Ruston, Louisiana

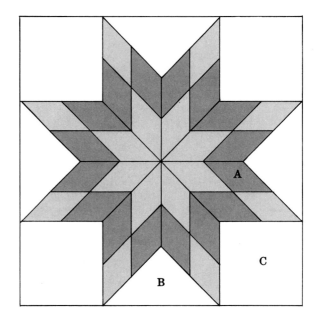

Mrs. Martin's pattern is one of the most popular of the old-time, traditional favorites. The colors she chose for her block are pale yellow, pale green, and brilliant orange, set against a white background.

Each block measures approximately 12 inches square (plus seam allowances). Mrs. Martin suggests the quilt be put together with alternating plain blocks. You would then have 21 pieced blocks and 21 plain blocks, and by setting the blocks 6 across and 7 down, and adding a 4-inch border, your quilt would measure approximately 80″ x 92″.

For one block you will need:
- A — 32 solid diamonds (8 orange, 16 green, 8 yellow)
- B — 4 white triangles
- C — 4 white squares (includes area of triangle B)

Allow ¼ inch for seams on all pattern pieces.

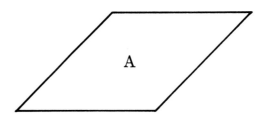

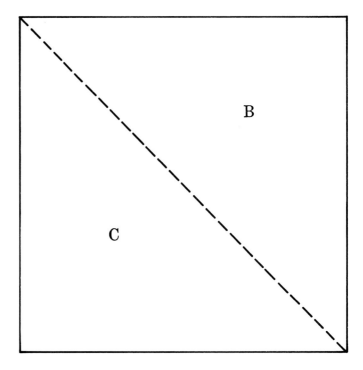

Path of Fans

Mrs. Robert H. Carr
Manchester, Tennessee

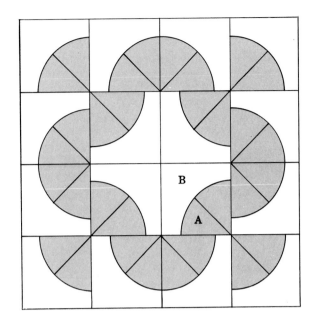

"This is a very easy quilt to piece," Mrs. Carr wrote, "and it is certainly pretty used with only two colors."

The block Mrs. Carr submitted in the traditional category will bear testimony to this fact. She chose a white background with a multicolor print of blue, purple, green, and yellow. The pattern is so pretty that one could choose almost any combination and come up with a beauty.

Mrs. Carr's block measures approximately 16 inches square (plus seam allowances), and it will take 30 blocks to make a quilt 80″ x 96″ when set 5 across and 6 down.

For one block you will need:
A — 32 print pieces
B — 16 white pieces
Allow ¼ inch for seams on all pattern pieces.

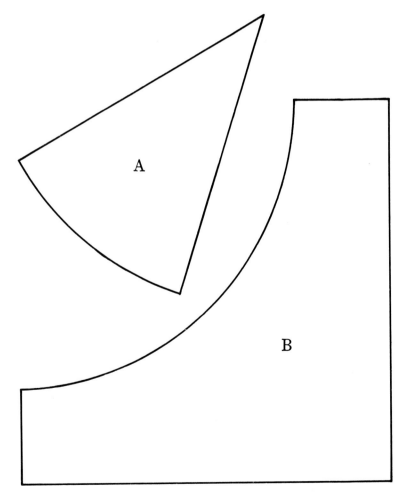

Star of Bethlehem

Mrs. A. Y. Reid

Russellville, Kentucky

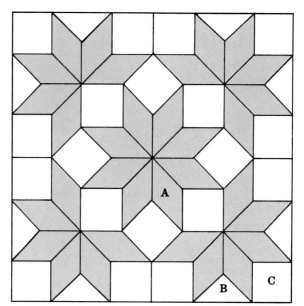

Of all the *Progressive Farmer* quilt block contestants, Mrs. Reid has a very special reason to have stars in her eyes. Since entering the contest, she has a wonderful new husband. "I still piece some," she wrote, "but haven't quilted since I got married 7 months ago."

Mrs. Reid is 75 years old, and she says her sight is getting bad. However, if you could see her beautiful star quilt block, all pink and white with specks of stardust in green and yellow, you wouldn't believe a word of it.

Twenty blocks, each about 17 inches square (plus seam allowances), will make into a lovely thing. Mrs. Reid wrote, "I didn't put it together with strips. I just sewed the squares together." With a 6-inch border, the quilt should measure 80" x 97".

For one block you will need:
   A — 32 print diamonds
   B — 8 white triangles
   C — 20 white squares
Allow ¼ inch for seams on all pattern pieces.

162

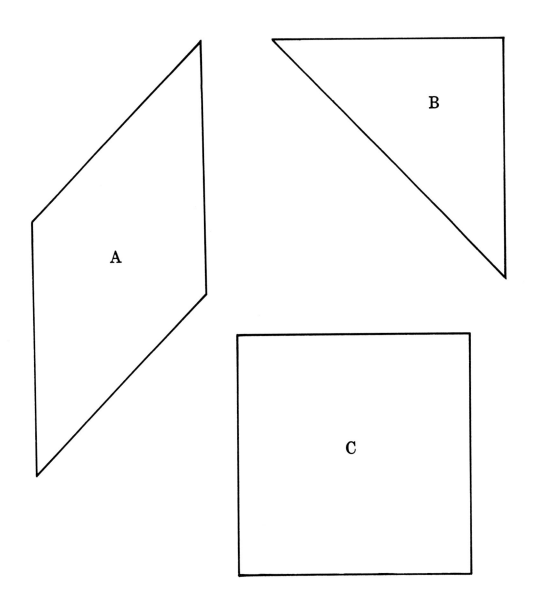

Pineapple

Mrs. George Steed
Lineville, Alabama

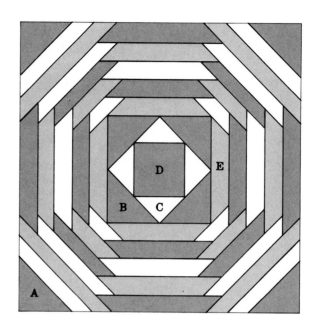

If you look carefully through this book, you will find a completed quilt of the *Pineapple* pattern made by Ruth Steed. It is one of the most beautiful quilts you will ever see, and when she makes one, she always buys her material so that each block will be alike.

A firm advocate of the quilt-as-you-go school, Mrs. Steed likes this pattern because she can pick up a block wherever she's going, and she can be working on it at any given time.

Although Mrs. Steed cuts the square in the center and the triangular pieces by pattern, she just tears the strips for the remainder of the block. "Be sure," she advises, "that you always use a material that will tear and tear well. It will save you countless hours when making a *Log Cabin, Pineapple,* or other strip-type quilts." Good advice, for it comes from a professional!

It is best to start in the center of the block and work toward the edges. Each strip is cut to the correct length after being attached. Mrs. Steed demonstrates how to do this in the quilt-as-you-go steps in the how-to chapter.

The finished block measures 11½ inches square (plus seam allowances) and a quilt 92″ x 103½″ will require 72 blocks set 8 across and 9 down.

For one block you will need:
  A — 4 rose triangles
  B — 4 rose triangles
  C — 4 print triangles
  D — 1 rose square
  E — 44 print strips
Allow ¼ inch for seams on all pattern pieces.

164

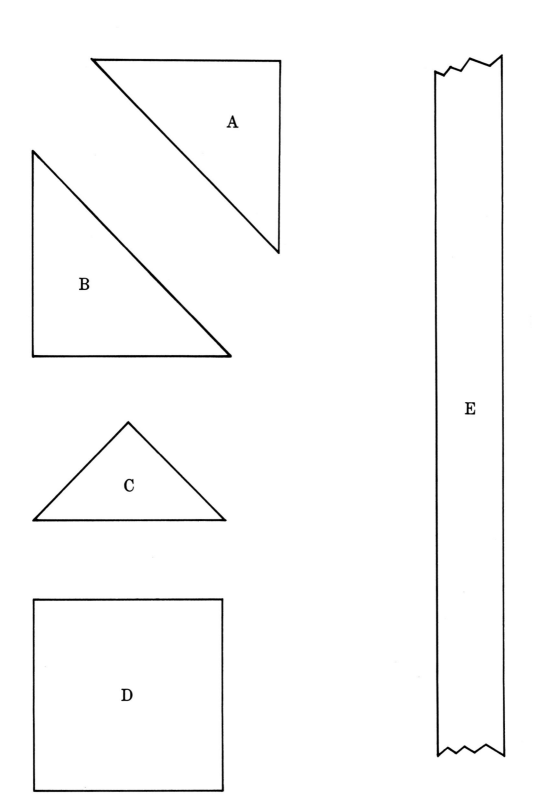

165

Flower Basket

Ruby T. Fleck
Vilonia, Arkansas

Apparently the quilting ladies who come from Arkansas really go in for the tiny patches. First Mrs. Venable, and now comes Mrs. Fleck with her gorgeous *Flower Basket.*

Using a sandpaper template, Mrs. Fleck's hexagonal design would present a challenge to anyone, and yet as difficult as it is to be certain you have each of the 6 corners a sharp point and each of the 6 sides a straight line, the *Flower Basket*-type quilt continues to be one of the most popular of all quilt patterns. If you use the paper technique on each of your hexagons as described in the how-to chapter, your pieces should fit together perfectly.

Mrs. Fleck said she took the pattern from a 1936 magazine, and that she has never made a quilt from this particular pattern. She used a bright yellow for the background of her quilt block, with rich dark brown hexagons for the basket. The flowers are various shades of rich dark solids.

To make a quilt from the *Flower Basket* pattern, you would need 307 hexagons for 1 block which measures about 17 inches square (plus seam allowances). You would need 30 blocks, 5 across and 6 down, for an 85″ x 102″ quilt. If you want to figure that in hexagons, it will amount to 9,210, give or take a few.

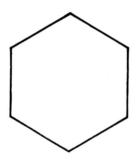

Seeing just the sample block makes the cutting all the more pleasureable, and when you see the wonderful mosaic effect achieved, you had better believe it's well worth the effort.

For one block you will need:
  307 solid hexagons —
  38 for the
  basket;
  13 leaves;
  22 flower
  petals;
  7 flower
  centers;
  227 back-
  ground
Allow ¼ inch for seams on all pattern pieces.

166

Dresden Plate

Ola L. Simmons
Belhaven, North Carolina

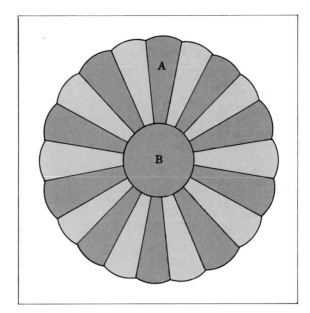

Dresden Plate is one of the truly old-time traditional patterns, and Ola Simmons knew that she had chosen an all-time winner when she submitted this entry in the *Progressive Farmer* Quilt Block Contest. For a colorful, exquisite quilt there just isn't a pattern that lends itself better than this one.

You will need to cut 42 solid material blocks, each 15 inches square (plus seam allowances). For the quilt backing you will need approximately 6½ yards of material. Using 6 blocks across and 7 blocks down, this will give you a quilt approximately 90″ x 105″. This particular pattern also lends itself to the use of an attractive border, using the petal motif of the plate as a design.

For one block you will need:
  A — 20 print pieces
  B — 1 solid circle
Allow ¼ inch for seams on all pattern pieces.

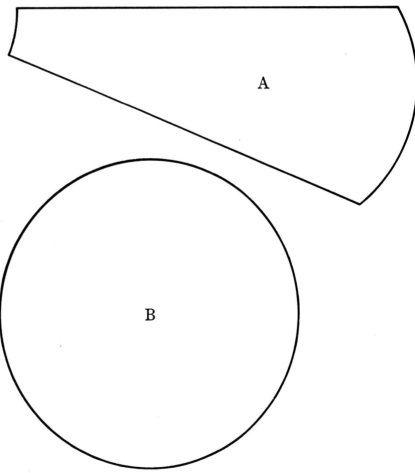

A

B

Flying Swallows

Jenny Lamoreaux
Shelbyville, Michigan

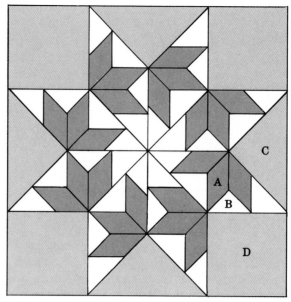

Jenny Lamoreaux is a quilt-book collector and works professionally on indexing, so she is more than interested in quilt patterns and their varying names. For her entry, she selected an old-time, traditional pattern.

Mrs. Lamoreaux had many helpful hints to offer, and she wrote that this particular pattern might lend itself to a modern setting by making the pattern pieces larger. In any event, it is an old-time favorite, dating from about 1800, and whether it is called *Falling Star, Flying Star, Flying Swallows,* or *Circling Swallows,* the wonderful effect of birds flying in a circle can't be minimized.

One very interesting observation is that Mrs. Lamoreaux prefers that pattern pieces be given without seam allowance. She feels that if she marks the seam lines directly on the fabric, this allows for more accurate piecing. It's a good point, and certainly a helpful suggestion.

To make a quilt approximately 96" x 108", you will need 8 blocks across and 9 down, each block measuring about 12 inches square (plus seam allowances). Add a border, using the dark solid or a double border of print with the

dark solid. This will increase the quilt size. When you get through, don't be surprised if you will have your own Capistrano all year long.

For one block you will need:
   A — 24 dark diamonds
   B — 32 light triangles
   C — 4 print triangles
   D — 4 print squares
Allow ¼ inch for seams on all pattern pieces.

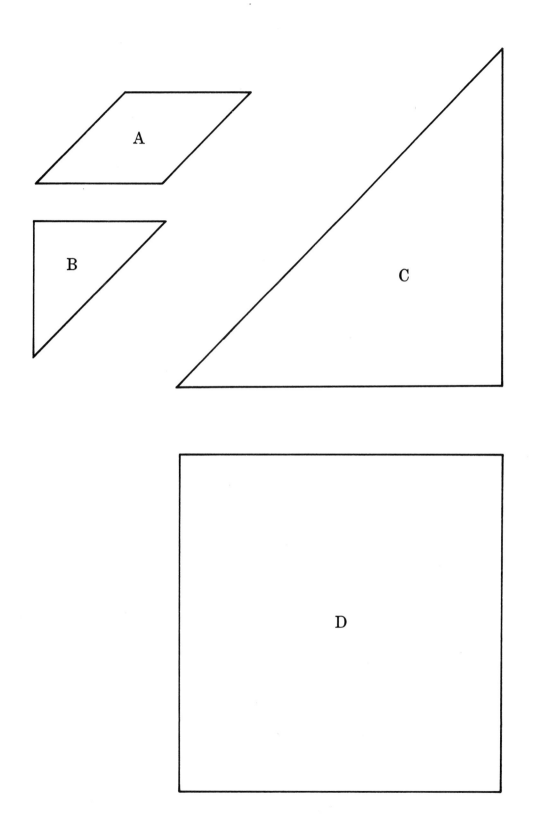

Jewels in a Frame

Mrs. Scott Williams
McAlister, Oklahoma

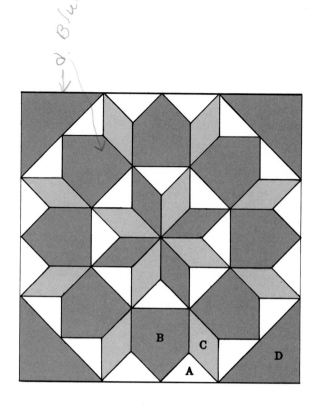

Mrs. Williams cut her pattern from one she saw several years ago in a magazine. According to a caption under the picture of the pattern, the designer was Mrs. Leo Wright of Center, Missouri.

The article suggested the use of rich jewel-tone fabrics to make the design, but Mrs. Williams chose parrot green, rose pink, and white for her colors, and the result speaks for itself.

Mrs. Williams said that her mother taught her to work with quilts when Mrs. Williams was about 7 years of age, and she has loved beautiful quilts since that time.

Mrs. Williams did not have directions to make a complete quilt, but each block measures approximately 16½ inches square (plus seam allowances), so a quilt 90½″ x 107″ would require 30 such blocks set 5 across and 6 down with a 4-inch border on all sides.

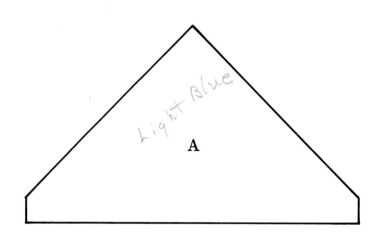

For one block you will need:
    A — 24 white triangles
    B — 8 green pentagons
    C — 16 solid diamonds
        (12 pink, 4 green)
    D — 4 green triangles
Each pattern piece includes a
¼-inch seam allowance.

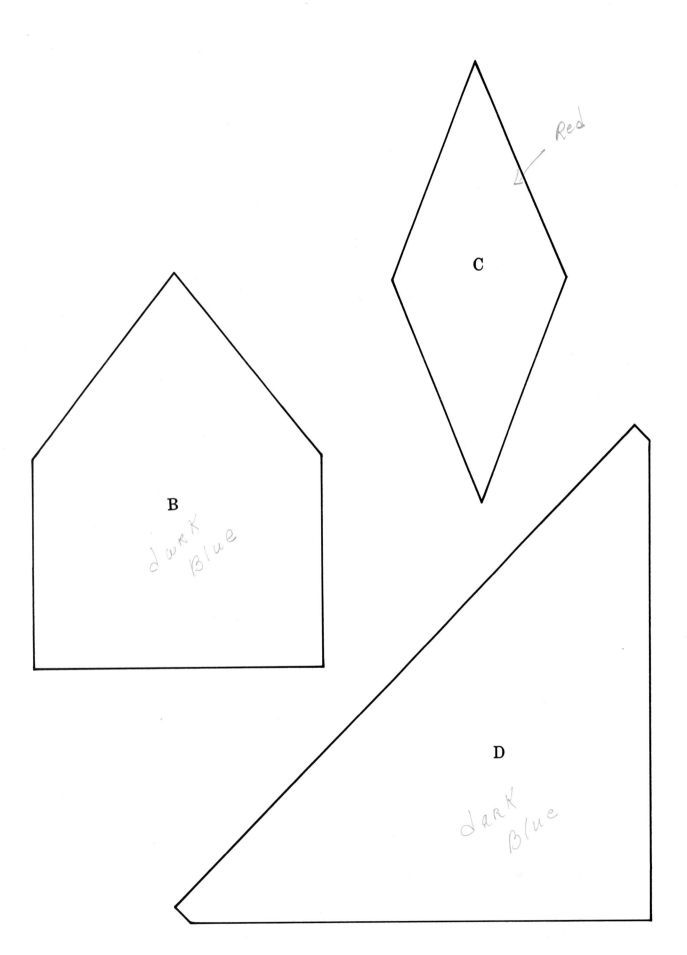

171

Delectable Mountains

Mrs. M. L. Gibbs
Cheriton, Virginia

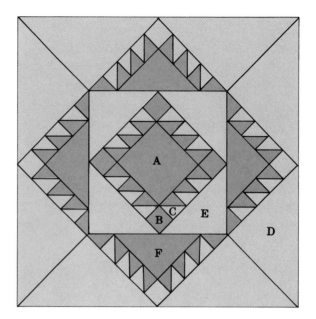

Mrs. Gibb's beautiful interpretation of one of the more traditional patterns is done in apple green and sunshine yellow — a delectable combination of colors.

Each block measures approximately 14 inches square (plus seam allowances). If 30 blocks are set 5 across and 6 down (you may wish to alternate pieced blocks with plain ones), with a 6-inch border, your quilt will measure approximately 82″ x 96″.

For one block you will need:
    A — 1 green square
    B — 8 small squares (2 green, 6 yellow)
    C — 72 small triangles (36 green, 36 yellow)
    D — 8 yellow triangles
    E — 4 yellow triangles
    F — 4 green triangles
Allow ¼ inch for seams on all pattern pieces.

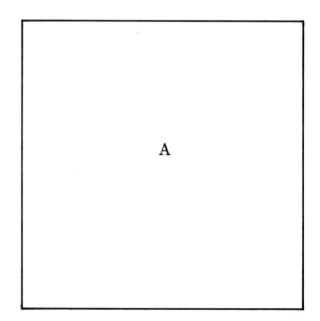

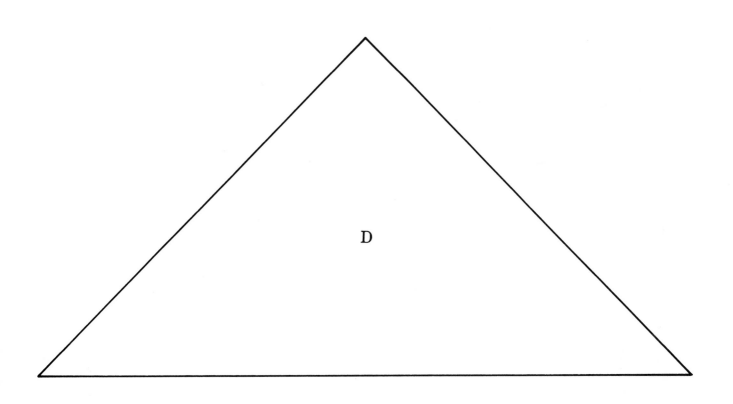

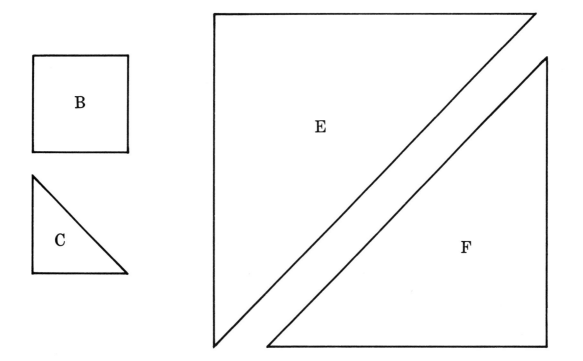

Sugar Loaf

Mrs. Myrtle Aldridge

Glen Allen, Alabama

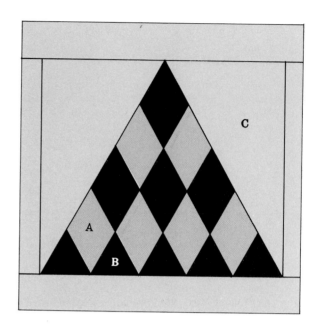

Before sugar was granulated, it came in cones wrapped in blue paper for shipment. The blue paper was saved, carefully, to be used for dyeing cloth a pretty blue color," Mrs. Aldridge wrote when she submitted this traditional entry in the quilt block contest.

She made *Sugar Loaf* in honor of her grandmother, who always wanted to make the pattern but never had the materials. The design is well over a hundred years old.

Each block measures 15" x 12½" (plus seam allowances). Thirty blocks set 5 across and 6 down with a 5-inch border will make a quilt 85" x 85". You may wish to give your quilt a different look either by alternating the pieced blocks with plain ones, or by turning every other block upside down.

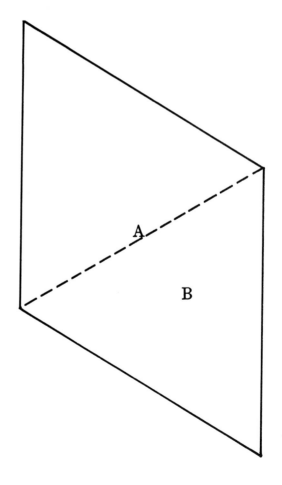

For one block you will need:
  A — 10 diamonds, 6 blue, 4 blue print (includes area of triangle B)
  B — 5 blue triangles
  C — 2 light triangles (pattern reduced — sides should equal 12½" x 7½" x 14½")
Allow ¼ inch for seams on all pattern pieces.

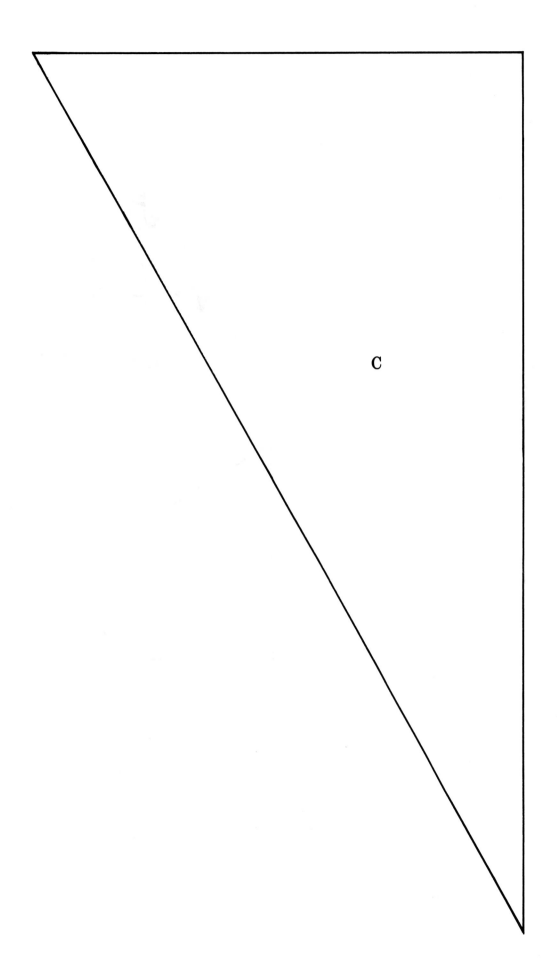

C

Single Irish Chain

Eleanor P. Myers
Barlow Bend, Alabama

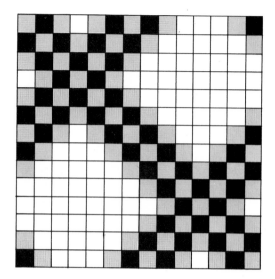

Mrs. Myer's beautiful pattern was handed down to her from her grandmother. "I had never pieced a quilt in my life," she said, "so the block I made for the contest was my first." This pattern is also known as *Triple Irish Chain.*

Single Irish Chain is a classic design involving tiny 2-inch squares (plus seam allowances). Mrs. Myers worked her entry in white, red floral print, and stunning crimson.

To make one 28-inch square block (plus seam allowances) you will need 196 2-inch squares. By setting 12 completed blocks 3 across and 4 down your quilt will measure 84" x 112".

For one block you will need:
196 squares — (82 white, 48 red print, 66 crimson)
Allow ¼ inch for seams on all pattern pieces.

176

The publishers acknowledge the award winners who helped make this book possible.

(Prize Winners)

TRADITIONAL

1st Mrs. C. C. Venable
England, Arkansas
Grandma's Square

2nd Mrs. O. W. Smith
Lepanto, Arkansas
Double Wreath

3rd Mrs. Irene Goodrich
Columbus, Ohio
Grandmother's Pieced Tulip

SPECIAL TRADITIONAL

1st Mrs. Annie Linder
Eastview, Kentucky
President's Wreath

2nd Bessie C. Bowman
Boones Mill, Virginia
Bride's Quilt

SPECIAL MODERN OR ORIGINAL

1st Gertrude Mitchell
Russell Springs, Kentucky
National Star

2nd Izola B. Marple
Buckhannon, West Virginia
The Strawberry

MODERN OR ORIGINAL

1st Mrs. Dorsey Zalants
Columbia, South Carolina
Oriental Bouquets

2nd Ruby Magness
Dermott, Arkansas
Grandma's Zinnia Basket

3rd Beatrice Gladys Baker
Zebulon, North Carolina
Green Pastures

(Honorable Mention)

Gertrude M. Abercrombie
Louisville, Alabama
Triple Sunflower

Mrs. Edna L. Adams
Hampton, Arkansas
Pansy

Minnie B. Allen
Huntington, New York
Dogwood

Cora Arrington
Hogansville, Georgia
Orange Blossom

Eula Askins
Peedee, South Carolina
Umbrella Girl

Mrs. Chester M. Ausherman
Walkersville, Maryland
*Great-Grandmother's Bridal
   Quilt*

Fannie Barnes
San Simon, Arizona
Miniature Yo-Yo

Leslie B. Barrow
West Blocton, Alabama
Flower Garden

Mrs. Velma Bass
McComb, Mississippi
Pansy

D. Elaine Baumgardt
State College, Pennsylvania
Grandpa's Handkerchief

Mrs. Fairy Bennett
Dawson Springs, Kentucky
Rocket Ship

Nellie Bennett
Buffalo, Kentucky
Sunshine and Shade

Mrs. Joe Bickham
Corpus Christi, Texas
Balloon Girl

Mrs. W. E. Black
West End, North Carolina
State Bird Quilt

Mrs. W. C. Blair
Russell Springs, Kentucky
Dahlia

Mrs. W. E. Blankenship
South Boston, Virginia
Star of Bethlehem

Eula Mae Bobo
Jacksonville, Texas
Butterfly Appliqué

Lucille Boggan
Albemarle, North Carolina
Flower Garden

Verdie Bolt
Ashland, Alabama
Tulip

Cora Bostick
Rotan, Texas
Orange Bud

Mrs. Carlton Brown
Fayette, Alabama
Star of Bethlehem

Mrs. W. K. Brown
Atmore, Alabama
Old-Fashioned Rose

Mrs. Grady Burrell
Canton, Georgia
Sunflower

Mrs. Tracy Butler
Bay City, Texas
Wishing Well

Ethel Byrd
Old Fort, North Carolina
Democrat Rose

Madge Byrd
Poyen, Arkansas
*Grandmother's Engagement
   Ring*

Margaret H. Call
Cape Girardeau, Missouri
Bed of Berries

Eloise Carr
Verona, Kentucky
Shocking

Mrs. Robert H. Carr
Manchester, Tennessee
Tulip

Euella M. Carter
Channelview, Texas
Twin Stars

Mrs. Leon Castleberry
Florien, Louisiana
Pineapple

Pauline Chaudoin
Tahlequah, Oklahoma
Squaw

Mrs. Z. E. Cheatham
Evergreen, Virginia
Tobacco Leaf

Mrs. R. M. Clack
Spring City, Tennessee
Heather Square

Lura Clark
Mount Vernon, Kentucky
Seven Sisters

Mrs. M. G. Clawson
Speedwell, Tennessee
Martha Washington Wreath

Mary P. Coats
Coats, North Carolina
Album Square

Mary Cole
Columbia, Kentucky
Democrat Banner

Mrs. Ida Mae Combs
Winchester, Kentucky
Crazy Quilt

Mrs. Arlene Cooper
Hillsboro, Kentucky
George Washington Plume

Miss Marianne Crawford
Clayton, Alabama
Road To Oklahoma

Mrs. Ora B. Curtis
Franklinville, North Carolina
Tulip Bed

Maybelline Dale
Westville, Oklahoma
Indian Squaw

Mrs. Fred Dallas
Union, Mississippi
Tree of Paradise

Mrs. Emory M. DeBusk
Urbanna, Virginia
Sunflower

Mrs. Louis Dilmore
Cottondale, Florida
Four T's

Elsie Doss
Gladehill, Virginia
Checkerboard

Mrs. Clyde Dunn
Hayden, Alabama
Tulip

Mary L. Dunn
Ashland, Nebraska
Spiked Tulip

Mrs. James E. Edmonds
Seguin, Texas
Pansy, Nine-Patch

Kristy Englert
Colorado Springs, Colorado
Umbrella

Mrs. N. A. Erickson
Benedict, Kansas
Fifty-Four Forty or Fight

Mrs. Paul Erwin
Cumberland, Virginia
Eight-Point Star

Mrs. Lilly Fiscus
Portland, Tennessee
Dutch Girl

Ruby T. Fleck
Vilonia, Arkansas
Flower Basket

Helen Fleenor
Chenoa, Kentucky
Stuffed Daisy

Azelie S. Fleitas
Loveland, Colorado
Lily of the Valley

Mrs. Richard Flinn
Scott, Louisiana
Hearts and Flowers

Mrs. Marshall Flint
Glasgow, Virginia
Little Dutch Girl

Mrs. Leta Flynn
Shawnee, Oklahoma
Indian Squaw

Kathleen Franks
Batesville, Arkansas
Old-Fashioned Rose

Mrs. Lucy Mae Franks
Clarksville, Texas
Triple Sunflower

Mrs. Gurney Frazier
Bardstown, Kentucky
Eternal Flame

Mrs. Herman Freeny
Carthage, Mississippi
Seven Star Texan

Elizabeth C. Frey
Bartlesville, Oklahoma
Windmill-Tulips

Mrs. Oma Garrett
Bolivar, Tennessee
Dove at the Window

Hazel Geveden
Arlington, Kentucky
Playhouse

Ealie Gibbs
Lafe, Arkansas
Blazing Star

Mrs. M. L. Gibbs
Cheriton, Virginia
Delectable Mountains

Lucille Gividen
Sulphur, Kentucky
The Drunkard's Path

Emma Goatley
Hardiburg, Kentucky
Star of Bethlehem

Grace Gordon
Manchester, Tennessee
Sweet and Low

Karen Grantham
Autryville, North Carolina
Butterfly

Mrs. John A. Hagelin
Lafayette, Louisiana
Tunisian Star

Mrs. U. G. Hall
Atmore, Oklahoma
The Iris Quilt

Mrs. Marie Harmon
East Point, Kentucky
Kitten in Basket

Irene G. Harper
Evergreen, Alabama
Feathered Star

Doris A. Harrell
Jefferson City, Tennessee
Tennessee Farm Boy

Mrs. Frankie Hatton
Dayton, Tennessee
Christ on the Cross

Mrs. S. W. Hawkins
Oswego, South Carolina
Jacob's Ladder

Bessie H. Hayes
Mount Vernon, Kentucky
Grandpa's Windmill

Mrs. Kate Heath
Carson, Virginia
Ship at Sea

Clara Z. Herndon
Horse Cave, Kentucky
Homespun

Mrs. W. R. Heasley
Little Rock, Arkansas
Improved Nine-Patch

Mrs. Edith Hewitt
Cleveland, North Carolina
Snoopy Dog

Mabel Hicks
Guymon, Oklahoma
The Tulips

Veda Hill
Batesville, Arkansas
Dutch Windmill

Cathie Hipsher
Rutledge, Tennessee
Lady's Puzzle

Frances Holveck
Cedar Hill, Texas
Sunflower

Nancy Howard
Ravenna, Kentucky
Cathedral Windows

Mrs. John Hunt
Nashville, Tennessee
Captive Beauty

Mrs. Ollie Hurt
Hazard, Kentucky
Lotts Creek Rose

Mattie Lou Infinger
St. George, South Carolina
Monkey Wrench

Mrs. R. C. Innis
Detroit, Texas
Box Knot

Amanda Jackson
Flat Lick, Kentucky
Mother's Love

Mrs. G. L. Jacobs
Boise City, Oklahoma
Solomon's Puzzle

Mrs. Linville Johnson
Thomasville, North Carolina
Heart

Mrs. Charles A. Johnson
Placid, Texas
Tulip

Martha Louise Johnson
Conowingo, Maryland
Chrysler Penta-Star

Mrs. Agnes Jones
Kosse, Texas
Communion Cup

Jayne Joshu
St. Louis, Missouri
Lattice Cross

Mrs. G. N. Kelly
Pollock, Louisiana
Rocky Road to California

Eunice A. Kentner
Clarksville, Tennessee
Seven Little Sisters

Minnie Mae Kimmer
Batesville, Arkansas
Poinsettia

Mrs. Lola King
Morristown, Tennessee
Poppy Wreath

Mrs. Flora Knapp
McIntosh, Alabama
American Beauty Rose

Mrs. Joe Korinek
Hallettsville, Texas
Wild Rose

Ida H. Layne
Dunlap, Tennessee
Ohio Rose

Lettie Lee
Cumberland Furnace, Tennessee
Pansy

Annie B. Leonard
Erick, Oklahoma
Church Lattice

Mrs. J. M. LeRoy
Stevenson, Alabama
Compass

Mrs. Mary Lewis
McMinnville, Tennessee
Turtle

Mrs. Amos Linder
Alpine, Tennessee
Hands All Around

Eula M. Long
Bloomington, Georgia
Mrs. Long's Rose

Carolyn Mary Loran
Munday, Texas
English Rose

Ora Loving
Gilmer, Texas
Grandma's Tulip

Minerva Lupton
Lowland, North Carolina
Monkey Wrench

Mrs. W. H. Mahaffa
Manchester, Tennessee
None Such

Mrs. Ongelene Marble
Elfrida, Arizona
Pieced Butterfly

Daisy Marcum
South Irvine, Kentucky
Butterfly

Mrs. E. G. Martin
Ruston, Louisiana
Blazing Star

Mrs. Fred H. Mayes
Marietta, Oklahoma
Magnolia

Mrs. S. B. Mayes
Decatur, Mississippi
Sunflower

Darria Maynard
Monterey, Tennessee
Young Man's Fancy

Mrs. V. H. McDonald
Lucedale, Mississippi
All-American Star

Elva V. Meeks
Geraldine, Alabama
X-Me-In

Zola M. Miller
San Saba, Texas
Orange Bud and Blossom

Marie Mills
Tahlequah, Oklahoma
Oklahoma Squaw Girl

Mrs. Blanche Mobley
Alachua, Florida
Double Wedding Ring

Mary F. Moore
Alvaton, Kentucky
Cathedral Window

Mrs. Nettie Griggs Moore
Wadesboro, North Carolina
Victory Sunflower

Jean Bell Mosley
Cape Girardeau, Missouri
Hollyberry

Mrs. Elizabeth G. Murray
Campti, Georgia
The Marguerite

Lizzie H. Neal
Holdsboro, North Carolina
Ohio Rose

Edith Nelson
Kenova, West Virginia
Butterfly

Mrs. Hallie M. Newberry
Gleason, Tennessee
Greenfield Village

Mrs. F. W. Osborne
Bentonville, Arkansas
Daisy

Mary Ostby
Somerville, Tennessee
Basket

Ruth K. Palmer
Niota, Tennessee
New York Beauty

Laura Parks
Simpsonville, South Carolina
Endless Trail

Mrs. Ouida Parsons
Tecumseh, Oklahoma
Red Sails 'n' Sunset

Mrs. C. R. Pitney
Cape Girardeau, Missouri
Progressive Education

Mrs. Fretta Pittman
Alta Loma, Texas
Road to White House

Mary Pope
Rose Hill, North Carolina
Flower Garden

Mrs. George Porter
Fayette, Alabama
Poto the Clown

Mrs. Rosa A. Rakes
Meherrin, Virginia
Rosa's Star

Mrs. Harman Rasnick
Nickelsville, Virginia
Kentucky Dahlia

Mrs. Van Ray
New Ulm, Texas
Rose of Paris

Minnie W. Reed
Cullomburg, Alabama
The Little Four-Point Save All

Mrs. H. E. Richter
Abernathy, Texas
Tumbling Blocks

Mrs. Hester Rofkahr
Clarksville, Arkansas
Rosebud

Mrs. Viva Rowland
Sims, Arkansas
Peace in the Valley

Mrs. Ethel Rucker
Rockwood, Tennessee
Pickle Dish

Ruby Rutan
Red House, West Virginia
The Great-Grandmother Quilt

Mrs. Edward Rutledge
Keysville, Virginia
Star and Cross

Bessie Seckman
Alma, West Virginia
Norway Pine

Mrs. David Seymor, Sr.
Rogersville, Tennessee
Dogwood Cluster

Sister Annene Siebenmorgen
Scranton, Arkansas
Pinwheel

Jennie J. Sigmon
Roanoke, Virginia
Triple Irish Chain

Mrs. Ernest L. Smith
Millwood, Georgia
Grandmother's Flower Garden

Lavina Smith
Marthaville, Louisiana
Fisher Boy

Mrs. Sue I. Smith
Kearny, Arizona
Mr. and Mrs. Clock

Mrs. J. C. Snyder
Groveton, Texas
Pansy

Annie Spitz
Fort Sumner, New Mexico
Friendship

Mrs. George Steed
Lineville, Alabama
Pineapple

Annie Stephens
LaFayette, Georgia
Star of Bethlehem

Savannah Stephens
Strunk, Kentucky
4-H Club

Mary Stufflebeam
Fayetteville, Arkansas
Pansy

Alberta Sullivan
Burlington, Kentucky
Wild Rose

Mrs. Louis Szabo
Tucumcari, New Mexico
Lincoln's Log Cabin

Flora Taylor
Baldwyn, Mississippi
Mounting Lilly

Mrs. Henry Teague
Eddyville, Kentucky
Martha Washington Star

Mrs. Audrey Thompson
Williford, Arkansas
Country Gardens

Maxine Thompson
Penhook, Virginia
Flower Garden

Mrs. Leola Treybig
Fayetteville, Texas
Springtime

Mercena Norton Tyson
Robertsdale, Alabama
Rocky Road to Dublin

Mrs. Annie B. Underwood
Radford, Virginia
Winding Blades

Mrs. Tom Yarbrough
Maysville, Georgia
Cherokee Squares

Ruth S. Yell
Gradford, Texas
Flower Garden

Ora Young
Morris Chapel, Tennessee
Flying Darts

Mrs. A. H. Walker
Cherry Valley, Arkansas
Circle Saw

Dorothy Walker
Evansville, Indiana
Aunt Kate's Flower Basket

Mrs. Pauline Walton
Pineland, Texas
Dogwood

Ruth Washington
Springville, Alabama
Rose Pattern

Mrs. Rex Watson
Valparaiso, Indiana
Double Wedding Ring

Oda May Webb
St. David, Arizona
A Bit of Spring

Mrs. V. V. Wieners
Hondo, Texas
Donkey

Mrs. Grace Wiggins
Century, Florida
Jonquil

Mrs. Ruth Williams
Rutledge, Tennessee
Alabama State Bird and Flower

Mrs. Scott Williams
McAlester, Oklahoma
True America

Bertha M. Wilson
Siloam Springs, Arkansas
Tulip

Mrs. Claude Wilson
Speedwell, Tennessee
Tulip

Mrs. Lizzie Wilson
Wapanucka, Oklahoma
Nine-Patch Star

Molean Wilson
Graham, North Carolina
Cathedral Windows

Myrtle Wilson
Olive Hill, Kentucky
Haystack

Mary Wingard
Lexington, South Carolina
Basket

Mrs. J. P. Womack
Bethpage, Tennessee
Garden Bouquet

Patti Woodall
Claremore, Oklahoma
Sleepwalking

Mrs. Ova Wright
Clovis, New Mexico
Old Star

Estella Zeigler
Redwood City, California
Flower Girl

Bibliography

"Art: In a Godless Age, an Escape from Materialism." *Birmingham News,* 24 February 1974.

Bacon, Lenice Ingram. *American Patchwork Quilts.* New York: William Morrow & Co., 1973.

Brooks, C. E. P. *Climate Through the Ages.* New York: McGraw-Hill Book Co., 1949.

"Climate and Man." *Yearbook of Agriculture.* Washington, D. C.: U.S. Department of Agriculture, U.S. Government Printing Office, 1941.

Colby, Averil. *Quilting.* New York: Charles Scribner's and Sons, 1971.

Finley, Ruth E. *Old Patchwork Quilts and the Women Who Made Them.* Newton Centre, Mass.: Charles T. Branford Co., 1957.

Gammell, Alice I. *Polly Prindle's Book of American Patchwork Quilts.* New York: Grosset and Dunlap, 1973.

Gurney, Gene. *Beautiful Washington D. C.* New York: Crown Publishers, 1969.

Gutcheon, Beth. *The Perfect Patchwork Primer.* New York: David McKay Co., 1973.

Hackett, Francis. *Henry the Eighth.* New York: Horace Liveright, 1929.

Hall, Carrie A., and Kretsinger, Rose G. *The Romance of the Patchwork Quilt in America.* New York: Bonanza Books, 1935.

Hall, Eliza Calvert. *A Book of Hand-Woven Coverlets.* Boston: Little, Brown & Co., 1912.

Hinson, Dolores A. *Quilting Manual.* New York: Hearthside Press, 1966.

Holstein, Jonathan. *Catalogue of the Smithsonian Institution Traveling Exhibition Service, 1972-1974.* New York: Paul Bianchini.

Holstein, Jonathan. *The Pieced Quilt.* Greenwich: New York Graphic Society, 1973.

Ickis, Marguerite. *The Standard Book of Quilt Making and Collecting.* New York: Greystone Press, 1949.

Laury, Jean Ray. *Quilts and Coverlets, a Contemporary Approach.* New York: Van Nostrand Reinhold Co., 1970.

Lewis, Alfred A. *The Mountain Artisans Quilting Book.* New York: Macmillan Co., 1973.

Lorant, Stefan. *Lincoln: A Picture Story of His Life*. New York: Harper Brothers, 1952.

Mahler, Celine Blanchard. *Once Upon a Quilt: Patchwork Design & Technique*. New York: Van Nostrand Reinhold Co., 1973.

The McCall Pattern Co. *McCall's How to Quilt It!* New York: The McCall Pattern Co., 1973.

The McCall Pattern Co. *McCall's Needlework Treasury*. New York: Random House, 1964.

"Mountain Co-Op Has a Rockfeller to Help Guide It." *New York Times,* 7 February 1974.

Newnes' Complete Needlecraft. London: Hamlyn Publishing Group Ltd., 1969.

Peto, Florence. *Historic Quilts*. New York: American Historical Society, 1939.

Stearns, Martha Genung. *Homespun and Blue: a Study of American Crewel Embroidery*. New York: Charles Scribner's and Sons, 1963.

Sunset Books. *Quilting and Patchwork*. Menlo Park, Calif.: Lane Books, 1973.

Swain, Margaret H. *Historical Needlework: a Study of Influences in Scotland and Northern England*. New York: Charles Scribner's and Sons, 1970.

Walters, John B. *Merchant of Terror*. New York: Bobbs-Merrill Co., 1973.

White House Historical Association. *The White House: An Historic Guide*. New York: Grosset and Dunlap, 1973.

Wooster, Ann-Sargent. *Quiltmaking: The Modern Approach to a Traditional Craft*. New York: Drake Publishers, 1972.

Index of Patterns

Appliqué Orchid Flower, 100
Aunt Eliza's Star, 148
Balloon Girl, 116
Bit of Spring, A, 95
Blazing Star, 160
Bride's Quilt, 86
Buck 'n' Wing, 130
Cathedral Windows, 92
Compass, 114
Delectable Mountains, 172
Democrat Banner, 88
Double Wedding Ring, 124
Double Wedding Ring, 158
Double Wreath, 70
Dresden Plate, 167
        Fancy, 110
Drunkard's Path, The, 108
Eight-Point Star, 141
Flower Basket, 96
Flower Basket, 166
Flower Garden, 127
Flying Swallows, 168
Four T's, 156
Grandma's Square, 68
Grandma's Zinnia Basket, 84
Grandmother's Engagement
    Ring, 150
Grandmother's Pieced Tulip, 76
Great-Grandmother Quilt,
    The, 134
Green Pastures, 78
Hands All Around, 154
Jack-in-the-Box, 144
Jewels in a Frame, 170
LeMoyne Star, 103
Lotts Creek Rose, 122
Martha Washington's Log
    Cabin, 98
Milky Way, 136
Monkey Wrench, 128
National Star, 80
New York Beauty, 138
North Carolina Rose, 126
Oriental Bouquets, 74
Our Village Green, 112
Path of Fans, 161
Persian Puzzle, 120
Pieced Star, 153
Pineapple, 164
President's Wreath, 72
Rosebud, 106
Single Irish Chain, 176
Star of Bethlehem, 162
Star and Stirrups, 109
Strawberry, The, 82
Sugar Loaf, 174

Sunflower, 132
Tobacco Leaf, 118
Tulip, 87
Turkey Track, 142
Virginia Star, 104
Wild Rose, 146
Wreath, 91